DATE DUE

AUG 0 5 1998

JAN 0 3 2017

6-24-19

The
Art of
Problem Posing

Second Edition

The
Art of
Problem Posing

Second Edition

Stephen I. Brown
*State University
of New York at Buffalo*
Marion I. Walter
University of Oregon

LEA LAWRENCE ERLBAUM ASSOCIATES, PUBLISHERS
1990   Hillsdale, New Jersey   Hove and London

Lawrence Erlbaum Associates, Inc., Publishers
365 Broadway
Hillsdale, New Jersey 07642

Lawrence Erlbaum Associates Ltd., Publishers
27 Palmeira Mansions
Church Road
Hove
East Sussex, BN3 2FA
U.K.

Library of Congress Cataloging-in-Publication Data
Brown, Stephen I.
    The art of problem posing / Stephen I. Brown, Marion I. Walter. — 2nd ed.
        p.   cm.
    Includes bibliographical references.
    ISBN 0–8058–0257–6. — ISBN 0–8058–0258–4 (pbk.)
    1. Problem solving.   I. Walter, Marion I., 1928–
QA63.B76   1990
511.3—dc20
                                                                89–17121
                                                                CIP

Printed in the United States of America
10   9   8   7   6   5   4   3   2   1

Contents

ACKNOWLEDGMENTS:
Second Edition

We wish to thank all our students who have, over the years, participated directly in our problem posing courses or who have experienced the spirit of such courses in our other more conventional settings. In addition to learning content per se, they were also encouraged to examine their fundamental beliefs both about the nature of mathematics and about their own learning. The reaction and participation of each group of students helped us to expand and refine our ideas about problem posing and solving, as well as about our role as teachers. The most valuable gifts they have given us have been the challenges to modify our emerging scheme—a scheme which is itself heavily rooted in the concept of modification.

Since the publication of the first edition of *The Art of Problem Posing* in 1983, the concept and language of problem posing has received more serious attention in curriculum and in research as well. We are grateful for the contributions our former students and colleagues have made in applying and elaborating upon the concepts developed in the first edition of *The Art of Problem Posing*. Because of the recent substantial contributions made by others, we are in the process of producing a book of readings based upon the use of our scheme by colleagues. References for some of these articles appear in our revised bibliography.

We are grateful to Mary Sullivan, Evelyn Anderson, and Mary Ann Green, all of whom spent many hours typing drafts at various stages of the first edition of the book, and we thank them for their patience, speed, and accuracy. In addition, we are grateful to Stephen I. Brown and Marion I. Walter for their heroic efforts in preparing the second edition of the book. Despite their better judgment, they both foolishly acquired word processing competency between the first and second printing of the book.

Julia Hough and Marcia Wertime offered constructive, valuable, and enthusiastic help in editing the first edition. Julia Hough encouraged us to exhibit and share the humor that the both of us enjoyed in working on this project. She then passed the mantle to Hollis Heimbouch and John Eagleson for assisting us in the preparation of the new edition. Jordan Brown's sketches for a revised cover and his suggestions of relevant cartoons helped us in achieving the latter two qualities.

Stephen I. Brown
Marion I. Walter
1990

THE FAR SIDE

Primitive think tanks

1

Introduction

Where do problems come from, and what do we do with them once we have them? The impression we get in much of schooling is that they come from textbooks or from teachers, and that the obvious task of the student is to solve them. Schematically, we have the following model:

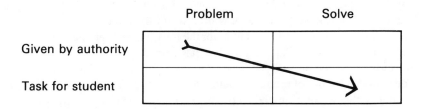

The purpose of this book is to encourage a shift of control from "others" to oneself in the posing of problems, and to suggest a broader conception of what can be done with problems as well.[1] Why, however, would anyone be interested in problem *posing* in the first place? A partial answer is that problem posing can help students to see a standard topic in a new light and provide them with a deeper understanding of it as well. It can also encourage the creation of new ideas derived from any given topic. Although our focus is on the field of mathematics, the strategies we discuss can be applied to activities as diverse as trying

---

[1]We shall not provide a formal definition of "problem" here, for the issue is more complicated than it might appear on the surface. For an effort to define the term see Gene P. Agre "The Concept of Problem," in *Educational Studies*, Vol. 13, No. 2, 1982, 121–142.

to create something humorous (as in *The Far Side* cartoon), attempting to understand the significance of the theory of evolution, or searching for the design of a new type of car bumper.

Have you ever thought, for example, of designing car bumpers that make use of liquid or that are magnitized, or shaped like a football, or capable of inflation upon impact? Or, have you thought of the possibility that they may be made of glass, the fragility of which might discourage people from driving recklessly or relying so heavily on the use of the automobile?

In addition to teaching explicit strategies for problem generation, there is an underlying attitude towards "coming to know" something that we would like to encourage. Coming to know something is not a "spectator sport," though standard textbooks, especially in mathematics, and traditional modes of instruction may give that impression. To say, rather, that coming to know something is a *participant* sport is to commit ourselves to a point of view requiring that we operate on and even modify the things we are trying to understand.[2] This attitude is central to the problem posing activities we shall develop in this book.

Our strategy for presenting ideas is generally an inductive one. Whenever possible, we attempt first to expose some problem posing issue through an activity that gets at it in an implicit and playful manner. After there has been some immersion in an activity we turn towards a reflection on its significance. We believe that it is necessary first to get "caught up in" (and sometimes even "caught" in the sense of "trapped by") the activity in order to appreciate what it is we are after. Such a point of view requires both patience and also an inclination to recover quickly from any embarrassment that results from being "caught." We believe the rewards will be worth the effort.

One way of gaining an appreciation for the importance of problem posing is to relate it to problem solving—a topic that has gained widespread acceptance (or rejuvenation, depending on your point of view). Problem posing is deeply embedded in the activity of problem solving in two very different ways. First of all, it is impossible to solve any novel problem without first reconstructing the task by posing new problem(s) in the very process of solving. Asking questions like, "What is this problem really saying?" or "What if I shift my focus from what seems to be an obvious component of this problem to a part that seems remote?" propels us to generate new problems in an effort to "crack" the original one.

Secondly, it is frequently the case that *after* we have supposedly solved a problem, we do not fully understand the significance of what we have done, unless we begin to generate and try to analyze a completely new set of problems. You have probably had the experience of solving some problem (perhaps of a practical, non-mathematical nature) only to remark, "That was very clever, but what have I really done?" These matters are discussed with examples in chapter 6.

---

[2]See John Dewey. *Reconstruction in Philosophy*. Boston, Beacon Press, 1957 for an analysis of such a conception of knowledge.

Often our formal education suppresses the relationship between the asking of questions and the coming up with answers. In a book which calls for a new perception of education, D. Bob Gowin comments:

> Recently a teacher was overheard to announce: "When I want your questions, I'll give them to you." . . . Much of school practice consists of giving definite, almost concrete answers. Perhaps boredom sets in as answers are given to questions that were never asked.[3]

More than boredom is at stake, however, when we are robbed of the opportunity of asking questions. The asking of questions or the posing of problems is a much more significant task than we are usually led to believe. The point is made rather poignantly in the story of Gertrude Stein's response to Alice B. Toklas, on Gertrude's death bed. Alice, awaiting Gertrude's legacy of wisdom, asked, "The answers Gertrude, what are the answers?"—Whereupon Gertrude allegedly responded, "The questions, what are the questions?"

The centrality of problem posing or question asking is picked up by Stephen Toulmin in his effort to understand how disciplines are subdivided within the sciences. What distinguishes atomic physics from molecular biology, for example? He points out that our first inclination to look for differences in the specific *content* is mistaken, for specific theories and concepts are transitory and certainly change over time. On the other hand, Toulmin comments:

> If we mark sciences off from one another . . . by their respective "domains," even these domains have to be identified not by the types of objects with which they deal, but rather by the questions which arise about them. . . . Any particular type of object will fall in the domain of (say) "biochemistry," only in so far as it is a topic for correspondingly "biochemical" questions.[4]

An even deeper appreciation for the role of problem generation in literature is expressed by Mr. Lurie to his son, in Chaim Potok's novel *In the Beginning:*

> I want to tell you something my brother David, may he rest in peace, once said to me. He said it is as important to learn the important questions as it is the important answers. It is especially important to learn the questions to which there may not be good answers.[5]

Indeed, we need to find out *why* some questions may not have good answers. For example, the questions might seem foolish or meaningless; or it might be that the questions are fundamental human questions that each of us might fight a

---

[3]D. Bob Gowin, *Educating.* Ithaca, NY: Cornell University Press, 1981, p. 127.
[4]Stephen Toulmin, *Human Understanding.* Princeton: Princeton University Press, 1977, p. 149.
[5]Chaim Potok, *In the Beginning.* New York: Knopf Publishers, 1976, pp. 295–296.

lifetime to try to understand; it may be that they are unanswerable questions because they are undecidable; it might also be, however, that our perspective on a problem is too rigid and we are blinded in our ability to see how a question might bear on a situation.

The history of every discipline—including mathematics—lends credence to the belief not only that it may be hard to distinguish good questions from bad ones in some absolute sense, but that very talented people may not be capable of seeing the difference even for a period of centuries. For a very long time, people tried to *prove* Euclid's fifth postulate:

Through a given external point, there is exactly one line parallel to a given line.

It was only during the past century that we began to realize that the difficulty in answering the question lay in the assumptions behind the question itself. The implicit question was:

How can you prove the parallel postulate from the other postulates or axioms?

It took hundreds of years to appreciate that the "how" was an unrecognized monster. If you delete the "how," the question is answerable (in the negative it turns out); if you do not do so, the question destroys itself as is the case with the question, "When did you stop beating your spouse"?

So far, we have tried to point out some intimate connections between the asking and answering of questions, and between the posing and solving of problems. There is a sense, however, in which problem generation is an important activity to pursue, even in the absence of uncovering "the right" solution, question or questions. In fact, there are many situations for which the concept of a right question is inappropriate. Imagine being given a situation in which no problem has been posed at all. A reasonable task might be to generate a problem or to ask a question, not for the purpose of *solving* the original situation (a linguistically peculiar formulation), but in order to create a problem that derives from the situation.

Suppose, for example, that you are given a sugar cube or the statement, "A number has exactly three factors." Strictly speaking, there is no problem in either case. Yet there is an infinite number of questions we can ask about either of the situations—some more meaningful than others, some more significant than others. However, it is rarely possible to tell in the absence of considerable reflection what questions or problems are meaningful or significant. We hope to persuade you in much of what follows, that things like significance and meaningfulness are as much a function of the ingenuity and the playfulness we bring to a situation as they are a function of the questions we ask. Frequently, even a slight turn of phrase will transform a situation that appears dull into one that "glitters."

There is another reason for asking interesting questions about a situation besides wanting to engage in creative activity or searching for answers: In looking at what happens when we pose new questions concerning an object—like a sugar cube or a statement that a number has exactly three different factors—we begin to "see" the object as we had never seen it before. We gain a deeper understanding of what constitutes a sugar cube or what it means for a number to be divisible by three factors. We shall further discuss issues of meaning and significance in chapter 3.

Sometimes the questions we ask about a phenomenon or a situation keep our perceptions of it intact. Sometimes, however, we end up drastically revising what we start with in the modifications we make. It is ironic that we sometimes come to "see" what is staring us in the face only after we "destroy" it in some way—at least mentally. The strategies behind such radical reconstruction of an object are discussed in chapters 4 and 5.

It is no great secret that many people have a considerable fear of mathematics or at least a wish to establish a healthy distance from it. There are many reasons for this attitude, some of which derive from an education which focuses on "right" answers. People tend to view a situation or even a problem as something that is *given* and that must be responded to in a small number of ways. Frequently people fear that they will be stuck or will not be able to come up with what they perceive to be the right way of doing things.

Problem posing, however, can create a totally new orientation towards the issue of who is in charge and what has to be learned. Given a situation in which one is asked to generate problems or ask questions—in which it is even permissible to modify the original thing—there is no *right* question to ask at all. Instead, there are an infinite number of questions and/or modifications and, as we implied earlier, even they cannot easily be ranked in an *a priori* way.

Thus we can break the "right way" syndrome by engaging in problem generation. In addition, we may very well have the beginnings of a mechanism for confronting the rather widespread feelings of mathematical anxiety.

This book then represents an effort on our part to try to understand:

1. What problem posing consists of and why it is important.
2. What strategies exist for engaging in and improving problem posing.
3. How problem posing relates to problem solving.

While problem posing is a necessary ingredient of problem solving, it takes years for an individual—and perhaps centuries for the species—to gain the wisdom and courage to do both of these well. No single book can provide a panacea for improving problem posing and problem solving. However this book offers a first step for those who would like to learn to enhance their inclination to pose problems. While this book does touch upon problem solving, it does so primarily as it relates to problem posing.

AUDIENCE

The Art of Problem Posing is written for a wide audience. It is intended for college math students, interested laypersons, present and future teachers of mathematics in middle school, in secondary school, and in higher levels of education. It also has implications for curriculum writers and for those who wish to do research on the power of problem posing and its relationship to a host of variables ranging from fear of mathematics to new strategies for teaching mathematics. We hope that it suggests directions for educators in fields other than mathematics as well. In fact, we are eager to continue to hear from practitioners in fields such as architecture, medicine, and engineering, who have viewed their work from a problem posing point of view, and who might find it useful to apply some of our techniques.[6]

Much of the book can be appreciated after having completed a high school mathematics program, although we occasionally assume a mathematics background roughly comparable to what is learned through the junior year in college.

Because we hope to appeal to a wide audience, we have intentionally selected a variety of mathematical topics and types of exposition to develop our points. We hope that people without extensive mathematical background will not be put off by what may occasionally appear to be technical approaches. On the other hand, we hope that people with a strong math background will appreciate the fact that material which appears simple may have considerable depth, and that much of what we discuss has implications for the most advanced mathematical material.

WAYS OF READING THE BOOK

While it would be helpful to explore many of the specific mathematical ideas presented in each chapter *before* attempting to follow the more general issues we bring up, it will not be a hindrance to skip a few examples during the first reading, should they seem too difficult.

We have stressed the importance of participation in coming to know and we hope that you will read this book in an active way. So, throughout the book, we ask a number of questions which we hope you will pursue. In fact, quite frequently, what we are after is a set of questions on your part and not primarily a set of answers to our questions.

Chapters 2 through 6 deal primarily with matters of problem generation and

---

[6]See Donald A. Schön's *The Reflective Practitioner*, New York, Basic Books, 1983 and *Educating The Reflective Practitioner*, San Francisco, Jossey-Bass, 1987 for a discussion of the need to re-conceptualize the preparation of professionals in all fields so as to view problem posing as a central phenomenon. His discussion of the training of architects in particular is quite enlightening.

should be of interest to the mathematics student and the layperson. Chapter 7 creates a pedagogical setting for an application of the point of view developed earlier. There we explore the concept of using an editorial board and suggest methods of incorporating it in the classroom in order to implement some of our problem posing strategies. This approach might be of interest to educators at all levels who would like to investigate a novel scheme for placing the student in a more active role. Especially given the emerging concept of writing across the disciplines (and not just in fields such as history and English), educators in all fields might wish to adapt parts of this approach in their own field of expertise.

ORIGINS OF THE BOOK

The material for this book has grown out of our experience in creating and team teaching courses on problem posing and solving at Harvard Graduate School of Education over two decades ago.[7] In addition to graduate students whose major concern was mathematics and education on both the elementary and secondary school level, on several occasions we had students at Harvard take our course who were preparing to be lawyers, anthropologists, and historians. Subsequently, we have taught variations of that course to both graduate and undergraduate students at numerous institutions, including Syracuse University, Dalhousie University, the University of Georgia, the University of Oregon, the University at Buffalo, and Hebrew University in Jerusalem. It is interesting for us to reflect on the fact that we did not originally perceive that we were creating something of a paradigm shift in focusing on problem posing. We thought rather that we were adding a new and rather small wrinkle to the already existing body of literature on teaching of problem solving that had been popularized primarily

---

[7]In addition to teaching courses on problem posing and solving we have published a number of articles dealing either directly or indirectly with several themes of this book. Some of the chapters reflect or incorporate material from these articles. The following co-authored pieces deal directly with the theme of problem posing: "What-If-Not," *Mathematics Teaching* (British Journal), 46, Spring 1969, p. 38–45; "What-If-Not? An Elaboration and Second Illustration," *Mathematics Teaching*, 51, Spring 1970, p. 9–17; "Missing Ingredients in Teacher Training: One Remedy," *American Mathematical Monthly*, April 1971, p. 399–404; "The Roles of the Specific and General Cases in Problem Posing," 59, *Mathematics Teaching*, p. 52–54; "Problem Posing and Solving: An Illustration of Their Interdependence," *Mathematics Teacher*, 70, 1, Fall 1977, p. 4–13.

Modifications of the first two pieces appear as part of chapter 4; a few sections of the third appear in Chapter 7; a small part of the fourth appears in chapter 3; a modified version of the last in chapter 6. The editors of each of the journals within which the material originally was published have granted permission to use what appears herein.

In addition to articles dealing with problem generation explicitly, we have each made implicit use of problem generation in several others. These pieces are mentioned in chapter 5 in the context of the development of relevant ideas.

by the work of George Polya. Over time, however, we have come to see that the activity of problem posing is capable of assuming a kind of centrality in its own right. Actually, it was the question we ask the reader to consider at the beginning of chapter 2 (about the Pythagorean equation) which launched us on the venture in the first place.

The emergence of a new interdisciplinary journal in 1987 entitled ''Questioning Exchange'' (edited by James T. Dillon from the University of California at Riverside) signals that the primacy of the problem or the question over the solution or the answer has begun to be appreciated in all fields of scholarship.[8]

Before embarking on our actual exploration of problem posing, we should mention that there will be a modicum of repetition of key ideas throughout the text. There are several reasons for this. First, and most importantly, these ideas are novel ones and it will most likely take a while to appreciate their force. Secondly (as we recommended in the previous section), you probably will skim the book at first and will not come across repetition until a second or third reading. Thirdly, we are now 110 years old (between the two of us) and we have become ever so slightly forgetful over the past few years. Fifthly, and most importantly, these ideas are novel ones and it will most likely take a while to appreciate their force!

What problems can you pose starting with the number 110?

---

[8]Though an important and ambitious undertaking, the journal was unfortunately short-lived. The last issue was published two years after the first.

2

Two Problem Posing Perspectives: Accepting and Challenging

$$x^2 + y^2 = z^2$$

After looking at the above equation, respond to the following:

"What are some answers?"

We have asked this question of our students and colleagues over the years. Before reading on, you might wish to answer it yourself. Jot down a few responses on a piece of paper, and we will then discuss the significance of the above question.

First Question Revisited

What was your reply to the question which opened this chapter? Answers will depend in part on your level of mathematical experience. People who have had very little experience with mathematics frequently respond, "Oh, that reminds me of some statement about right triangles, but I can't remember it exactly."

Those who have had more experience with mathematics sometimes respond with a list like the following:

3, 4, 5
5, 12, 13
8, 15, 17.

Then they remark that they know there are a few other such number triples but they cannot recall them.

Among those who have had a great deal of experience, we have frequently received the above and, in addition, a comment about the potential length of such a list. They suggest how many triples there are and, occasionally, either recall or attempt to generate a formula for them.

People who know more about real or imaginary numbers are often pleased when, almost in a sense of amusement, they produce the following sets of numbers:

$$2, 3, \sqrt{13} \quad \text{or} \quad i, 1, 0.$$

Now look back at all the above responses. Notice that something very significant has happened. All the responses to, "What are some answers?" assume that a question has been asked by the equation itself. Furthermore, they assume that the specific question asked when we wrote "$x^2 + y^2 = z^2$" was: "What are some integer solutions (or perhaps real or imaginary ones)?"

Notice, however, that "$x^2 + y^2 = z^2$" is not in itself a question at all. If anything, it begs for you to *ask a question* or to *pose a problem* rather than to answer a question.

It may look as if we are splitting hairs or that we have pulled your leg by setting a trap. Our experience indicates, on the contrary, that we are getting at something important. Perceiving $x^2 + y^2 = z^2$ only as an equation that requires solving for x, y, and z reveals a very limited perspective. As you read on, you will see that the issues we are getting at open up vast new possibilities for learning in general and for learning mathematics in particular.

There is a myth that it is the role of the expert or authority (textbook, teacher, research mathematician) to ask the questions and for the student merely to answer them. Of course, it is considered good pedagogy to encourage students to ask questions, but they are usually questions of an instrumental nature—questions that enable teachers to pursue their pre-conceived agendas.

Frequently students are encouraged to ask questions which enable them to better follow well-trodden terrain that has been laid out not only by their teacher, but by the mathematics community at large. In grade school, for example, teachers encourage children to ask questions to make sure that they understand existing procedures.

A typical interchange might be:

Teacher: "Do you understand how to add two-digit numbers?"
Johnny: "Did you say we have to add from right to left?"
Teacher: "Good question. Yes. Let me show you what happens if you did it from left to right. Let's do a problem.

$$\begin{array}{r} 95 \\ + 87 \\ \hline \end{array}$$

"Let's find the sum by adding from left to right but carrying in the way I showed you.

$$
\begin{array}{r}
9\ 5 \\
+\ 8{,}7 \\
\hline
7\ 1\ 3
\end{array}
$$

"You see, you get the answer 713, but you know it must be wrong because you can tell the answer must be less than 200."

Note that the teacher has not approached the question in a completely arbitrary way, for a reason has been offered other than the teacher's authority for preferring one method over another. Furthermore, it is possible that Johnny's question could lead to some interesting exploration. For example, a teacher could encourage a student to investigate modified strategies for which we could get the correct answer by adding from left to right. Or the teacher and student could explore the extent to which the notation itself imposes one algorithm over another. Nonetheless, students and teachers do not usually ask questions for such purposes; rather, they are interested in making sure that their students understand and can execute what is expected of them.

Such an atmosphere neither leads to understanding the significance of an activity or a procedure, nor does it contribute to the development of a sense of autonomy and independence. In contrast, problem posing can give one a chance to develop independent thinking processes. Most people have been denied this ingredient in their learning—especially in their mathematics classes. It is the ability to pose problems rather than merely to ask procedural questions, such as the one above, that is a central component in the development of an autonomous person.

A SECOND LOOK AT $x^2 + y^2 = z^2$

Reconsider $x^2 + y^2 = z^2$. Now let us ask not, "What are some *answers?*" but, "What are some *questions?*" Before reading on, list some of your own questions.

Here are some of the responses people have given at this early stage:

1. Who first discovered it?
2. Are the solutions always integers?
3. How do you prove it?
4. What's the geometric significance of this?

Loosening Up

In order to loosen up your own thinking processes further at this point and to give them free reign, write down any ideas, not necessarily questions, that occur to you when you look at and think about $x^2 + y^2 = z^2$. No holds barred! We are asking you to free associate and write down any ideas you have.

Some Typical Observations

Did you write down any statements or questions of the following types?

1. Some famous right triangles are 3, 4, 5; 5, 12, 13; and 8, 15, 17.

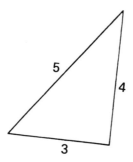

2. The Greeks used knots on a rope to make a right triangle.

3. You can use it to introduce irrational numbers.
4. This is associated with the Pythagorean Theorem.
5. It's the only thing I remember from geometry.
6. It reminds me of ladders against a wall.

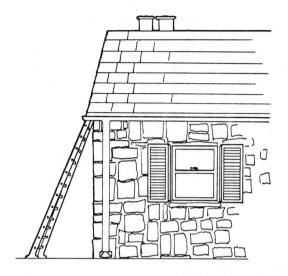

7. How do you find more triplets satisfying $x^2 + y^2 = z^2$?
8. Is 3, 4, 5 considered different from 6, 8, 10 or from 30, 40, 50?
9. It has to do with squares on the sides of a right triangle.

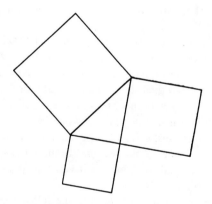

10. What good is any of this?

Notice that even in this small sample of observations, we have a few new ideas for $x^2 + y^2 = z^2$: Namely, that it can deal with triangles; that it has a history; and that there are applications of it.

A NEW PERSPECTIVE

We are not yet done with the equation $x^2 + y^2 = z^2$. In fact, we have hardly begun. Compare the kinds of questions just mentioned with the following list of questions also using $x^2 + y^2 = z^2$ as a point of departure:

1. For what integral values of x, y, z is it true that $x^2 + y^2 < z^2$?
2. For what values is it true that $x^2 + y^2 = 1 + z^2$?
3. What happens to the Pythagorean Theorem if the triangle is not a right triangle? That is, suppose the right angle is replaced by a 60° angle. How is $x^2 + y^2 = z^2$ affected?
4. For what 60° triangles (i.e., triangles with at least one 60° angle) can you find three sides that are all integers?
5. If you replace the squares on each side of the triangle by rectangles that are not squares, do the areas on the legs ever add up to the area of the rectangle on the hypotenuse?
6. Is there a three-dimensional analogue for the Pythagorean Theorem?
7. What analogy is there for four-sided figures?

A Reflection on the Preceding Questions

What are the differences between the thinking shown in the preceding set of questions and the thinking shown in questions and observations we made in the previous subsections?

There are many ways of answering this question. In making such comparisons what we see is very much a function of our idiosyncratic experiences and of the kinds of lenses we are accustomed to use. We could, for example, try to compare the questions with regard to their degree of generality or the sense in which they call for algorithms. Since you do not know where we are headed at this point, it is probably very difficult to get a grasp on what we see as a *salient* difference between the above seven questions and those that precede them. Nevertheless we urge you to take a stab. Compare the section "Some Typical Observations" with the section "A New Perspective" and see if you can find some differences that mean something to you.

Perhaps you have observed differences of the following kinds:

1. Degree to which you strive only for *solutions* of the equation $x^2 + y^2 = z^2$.
2. Degree to which you search for literal or narrow interpretation of the equation $x^2 + y^2 = z^2$.
3. The degree to which you risk asking questions for which you may not have a method of solution.

4. The style in which you interpret the mathematics, for example, geometrically or algebraically.

In addition to these four categories (and many others), there is one that has significantly influenced our thinking about problem posing. It is a bit subtle and took us a while to appreciate, although after realizing it, it is hard to imagine that there was a time we did not see it.

5. The degree to which one "accepts" the given.

Notice that sometimes we have essentially accepted the given—in this case $x^2 + y^2 = z^2$ and its relationship to the Pythagorean Theorem—and sometimes we have *challenged* the given in order to ask new questions. We do not, in the latter case, take the given for granted. Rather, the given is a starting point for investigations that modify it. For example, instead of considering $x^2 + y^2 = z^2$ and squares on the sides of right triangles, we asked about such forms as $x^2 + y^2 = 1 + z^2$ and we replaced squares with rectangles. Though problem posing using each of these perspectives is valuable and necessary, it is *challenging* the given which frequently opens up new vistas in the way we think. Only after we have looked at something, not as it "is" but as it is turned inside out or upside down, do we see its essence or significance.

We have refined this notion of challenging the given into a strategy that can be learned, and we have coined the phrase "What-If-Not?" to describe it. It is a second phase of problem posing after the earlier one of *accepting* the given. Ironically, we first begin to gain a deeper understanding of something when we modify it into something else. It is worth keeping in mind that though it is possible to learn a strategy for challenging the given, it is not possible to guarantee (by using any particular procedure) that we will capture those phenomena we later perceive to be most significant. It takes not only insight but courage and sometimes totally new world views for anyone to find significant challenges. Merely looking for something to challenge will not guarantee that we will find it. The fact that it has taken such a long time even to *realize* that there were attitudes to be challenged concerning full-time employment, leisure time, aging, race, and sex roles suggests how difficult it is to perceive that there are things to challenge.

In the next chapter we explore the first phase of problem posing—where we accept the given—and in chapter 4, in which we introduce the second phase, the "What-If-Not" approach.

3

The First Phase of Problem
Posing: Accepting

In this chapter we will explore how we might broaden our outlook on problem posing, by sticking with the given in our exploration. We begin with a number of different kinds of examples. They will provide a concrete context in which we can reflect on issues related to this first phase of problem posing.

STICKING TO THE GIVEN: SOME EXAMPLES

Example 1. A "Real Life" Situation: Supreme Court Judges

Several years ago a speaker gave a talk at a meeting of mathematics educators. He began with the following observation:

> There are nine Supreme Court Justices. Every year, in an act of cordiality the Supreme Court session begins with each judge shaking hands with every other judge.

He then asked the audience what the obvious question was in this set-up. The task appeared to the speaker to be so obvious that he treated his query as a rhetorical question, answered it himself and proceeded with the talk. What do you think the question was? Well, you might have guessed that his question was, "How many handshakes were there altogether?"

Many of us are blinded to alternative questions we might ask about any phenomenon because we impose a context on the situation, a context that frequently limits the direction of our thinking. We all do this to some extent because we are influenced by our own experiences and frequently are guided by specific goals (e.g., to teach something about permutations and combinations), even if we may not be aware of having such goals.

The ability to shift context and to challenge what we have taken for granted is as valuable a human experience as creating a context in the first place. With this in mind, what else might you ask in the case of the Supreme Court situation? Some of the questions people have asked, after considerable thought were:

1. Would you predict an even or an odd number of handshakes?
2. Can you come up with a lower limit to the number of handshakes?
3. Is the handshaking task one that is even possible to perform?[1]
4. Can you come up with a number that is an upper limit to the number of handshakes before attempting an exact calculation?
5. Does a handshake between two people count as one or as two handshakes?
6. If it takes three seconds to shake hands, what is the least amount of time necessary for all the handshakes?
7. If three justices arrive late, how many handshakes still need to be made?
8. If they are sitting two feet apart on one long bench, what is the least amount of walking needed in order for them all to shake hands?
9. If a group of four judges have shaken hands and the remaining five have already done so, how many handshakes remain?

You may have noticed that despite our efforts at extending the range of questions, we have narrowly confined all our questions to mathematical ones. Had we not intended to focus on mathematics, we might well have included such questions as:

10. Does the handshaking have an effect on subsequent cordiality?

Or heretically, we might respond:

11. Isn't that nice? or
12. Who cares?

Though our focus is mathematical, these non-mathematical comments and questions raise an important issue concerning the concept of significance, which we will discuss towards the end of this chapter.

---

[1]This is not an unreasonable question. If we suggested, for example, that four people should shake hands with each other but no one should shake hands an even number of times we would find this task impossible to fulfill.

Example 2. A Geometric Situation: An Isosceles Triangle

Let us take an example that seems so simple we might doubt that it could lead to new ideas. Assume that we have a triangle in which two sides are equal in length—an isosceles triangle. What questions could you ask?

Students who have studied geometry often find the following to be "obvious" questions.

1. Why is it called isosceles?
2. How can you prove that the base angles are "equal"—i.e. congruent?

List some other questions, without taking into consideration whether or not you are familiar with the answer. In listing your own questions, you might find it worthwhile to ask yourself what made you think of them. Below are a few additional questions that could be asked:

1. How might we classify isosceles triangles? We might, for example, classify them with regard to their vertex angles (e.g., obtuse, right, acute) or the ratio of the lengths of base to side. What other ways can you think of?
2. What types of symmetry does an isosceles triangle have?
3. If one angle of an isosceles triangle is twice another, is the shape of the triangle determined?
4. What relationships exist among the exterior angles of the triangle? How do the exterior angles relate to the interior angles?
5. What was it that encouraged people initially to investigate isosceles triangles?
6. What other figures can you make with congruent isosceles triangles? Using two of them? Using three of them? Others? What geometric figures have been created by replicating an isosceles triangle below? Can you make others?

7. Can you make a collection of congruent isosceles triangles into a bicycle hub?

The isosceles triangle is particularly interesting, for unlike the Supreme Court situation, the concept is part of the standard curriculum. Ironically enough, those who have most recently been exposed to a course in geometry (at almost any level) tend to find great difficulty coming up with much more than observations relating the equality of lengths to the equality of angles, while those who have not studied the subject, or perhaps consider themselves "weak" in mathematics, tend to come up with more robust questions and observations like questions 5–7. What this tells us is that focusing on a topic by studying it in some formal or official sense (finding out what the culture has to say about it) sometimes has the effect of narrowing rather than expanding our view. One way of regarding our schemes for problem generation is as a sensitizing kit to prevent the study of any well-established scheme from narrowing our perspective.

Example 3. Concrete Material: Geoboards

Problem posing can be initiated with almost anything—definitions, theorems, questions, statements, and objects, just to list a few possibilities. Let us turn next to a concrete material, one that has become popular in school mathematics—the geoboard (see Figure 1[a]). This one is a square wooden board with 25 nails in it. It is called a five-by-five board. As is customary, we can make shapes with rubber bands as shown in Figure 1(b).

The geoboard has an appeal to the uninitiated student as well as to the sophisticated one. People have written many books and guides for its use. What would you do with it? Give yourself a minute to think.

Most of the books suggest particular questions or problems with varying amounts of detail and at various levels of sophistication. A standard elementary task would be:

1. Using rubber bands, make a number of different shapes on the board.

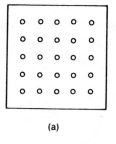

(a)

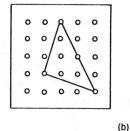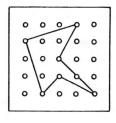

(b)

FIG. 1.

A harder problem might be:

  2. Taking the smallest square as a unit, find the area of shapes created in answer to *Task 1*.

Significantly more sophisticated questions would be:

  3. Given only the number of nails inside and on the boundary of any shape created in Figure 1(b), can you determine what the figure looks like? What the area is?[2]
  4. How many non-congruent squares can you make on a five-by-five geoboard?

Notice that in all these questions or tasks, the *given,* the geoboard, was accepted as is. Although we could make even the above list almost endless, we will open up even more ways of asking questions about a geoboard in chapter 4 when we approach the task from the perspective of *challenging* the given.

Example 4. Looking at *Data:* Primitive Pythagorean Triples

In Chapter 2, we saw that $x^2 + y^2 = z^2$ often triggers "the answers" 3, 4, 5; 5, 12, 13; 7, 24, 25; even before a question has been asked. This time let us accept the assumed question, "For what whole numbers is it true that $x^2 + y^2 = z^2$?" A partial list of ordered primitive Pythagorean triples[3] is shown in Table 1.

   Starting with this table what questions, observations, or hypotheses can you make after studying the data?

---

[2]See Niven, I. and Zuckerman, H. "Lattice Points and Polygonal Area." *American Mathematical Monthly,* Vol. 74, No. 10, Dec. 1967, pp. 1195–1200 for a rigorous analysis of this problem (which can be analyzed intuitively by many junior high school students). See also Yaglom, I. and Yaglom, A. *Challenging Mathematical Problems,* Vol. 2. Holden Day, 1967 (San Francisco). The actual formula for the area A is $A = \frac{1}{2}b + i - 1$ where i is the number of nails inside the shape and b the number of nails on the boundary, assuming the unit of area is the square s below. There, for example, i = 2, b = 7. Then, according to this formula, A should equal $\frac{1}{2} \cdot 7 + 2 - 1 = \frac{9}{2}$. Verify that this answer is correct without using this formula.

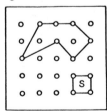

[3]Pythagorean triples x, y, z are said to be primitive if x, y, z are relatively prime. That is, they have no factors other than 1 in common. Thus 6 and 7 are relatively prime, but 6 and 8 are not.

TABLE 1
A Partial List of Ordered
Primitive Pythagorean Triples

x	y	z
3	4	5
5	12	13
7	24	25
8	15	17
9	40	41
12	35	37

One of our classes came up with the following list.

1. It appears that sometimes $z = y + 1$, sometimes $z = y + 2$.
2. Is z always odd?
3. Is z always either a prime or divisible by 5?
4. x and y seem to have different parity (i.e., one is odd and the other even).
5. Is y always divisible by 4 or 5?
6. If x is odd, $z = y + 1$.
7. If x is even, $z = y + 2$.
8. Every triple has one element divisible by 5 and one by 4.
9. It looks as if x will run through many of the odd integers.
10. Can you get a triple for any value of x you choose? What about y? z? Which ones can't you get?
11. Will every multiple of 5 occur somewhere in the table?
12. It looks as if $z = y + 1$ implies $y + z = x^2$.
13. If x is even, $z + y = x^2/2$.
14. z's appear all to be of the form $4n + 1$.
15. Listing only those triples for which $z = y + 1$, is it always true that any two y's differ by the same amount as any two z's?
16. For a fixed x, are y and z always unique? Same with a fixed z?

Our point in choosing the Pythagorean triples as data is to show that such data are frequently a wealthy source for generating new questions. The issue goes deeper than that, however. People with a mathematical bent who take a look at the partial list of triples frequently focus exclusively on the search for some formula that might generate the entire list. Though some of the questions we have listed above have the possibility of heading us in that direction, not all of them do. That is, there are many surprising observations—like number 8 on the list—which appear to have no obvious connection with a search for a formula to create all triples.

Example 5. Simple Number Sequence

There is something mysterious about the data in Table 1 for most people who first stumble upon them. Even if you suppress the desire to figure out how the sequence triples might be generated by a formula, there is still a nagging puzzlement about the source of it all, and we tend to be pulled in that direction even if we allow for occasional diversions. But even simple data whose generating formulas are not in question can be a source of surprise and marvel, provided we assume a problem posing stance. Suppose we list a sequence such as 9, 16, 23, 30, 37, 44, 51, 58, ... What questions and observations come to your mind?

A possible list might include:

1. The difference between the numbers is 7.
2. The first two numbers are perfect squares. Are there more perfect squares in this sequence? When does the next one occur? How many are there?
3. What is the nth term?
4. If we subtract 2 from each number, it is just the 7 times table.
5. If we add 5 to each number it is almost the 7 times table!
6. Two numbers of the list given are prime. As you extend the sequence will there be an infinite number of primes?
7. The numbers alternate between ones that are odd and even.
8. There is a number in the sequence that is divisible by 2, a number divisible by 3, one by 4, one by 5, by 6, but not one by 7. Is 7 the only exception?
9. Do all digits from 0 to 9 occur in the units place? Tens place?
10. Is there a pattern to the last digits?
11. Can you tell quickly if 1938 appears in the list?

As in the case of the isosceles triangle example, here is something that is included in standard curriculum under the topic of arithmetic progressions. Blinded by the realization that some things are already well-known about this kind of sequence (that is, how it is created and how it grows), many people incorrectly conclude that there is nothing more to find out. Questions such as numbers 6, 8, 9, and 10 however, suggest that beneath the surface of our pedestrian sequence we can find some surprising implications. While we may have explored arithmetic sequences in general, we have not explored this one *in particular*, and every special case has a world within it that is not covered by the general investigation.

SOME REFLECTIONS ON PHENOMENA TO
INVESTIGATE

What have we explored so far in this chapter? Specifically, we have looked at five examples, but it would help to find a way of classifying them in order to help us come up with many others.

Let us begin by asking what we normally select for carrying out an investigation. Since, in the eyes of most people who design curriculum, mathematics is about propositions, the starting point (sometimes disguised or diluted) is usually a collection of statements—definitions, axioms, theorems, and the like. We make statements and try to prove them.

What else might we use other than propositions? Look at Examples 2 and 3 of this chapter. What we have in each case is an object—one of them abstract and the other concrete. In Example 1, we have something closer to a situation. Objects and situations then may be helpful starting points for generating new questions.

We have also selected data as a starting point for investigation in Examples 4 and 5. In example 5 the data are generated explicitly by a formula ($y = 7x - 2$ for x a natural number); in example 4 they are generated by an implicit formula ($x^2 + y^2 = z^2$).

Once we have acquired data by whatever method, we can view the data as taking on a life of their own. We can thus focus on more than the origin of the data. That is, we are in a position to ask questions that do not necessarily focus upon methods of generating the data. Now that we are aware of the variety of objects about which we might pose problems, what strategies might we use to generate questions?

STRATEGIES FOR PHASE-ONE PROBLEM GENERATION

Things to do with Phenomena

Exploration of something, whether it be a concrete object (geoboard), an abstract object (an isosceles triangle), data or a theorem itself, can take many forms. What have we done so far that enables us to generate problems? We have done more than just ask questions. Sometimes we have made observations. At other times we came up with conjectures. Frequently these observations or conjectures themselves can lead to questions and vice versa.

Let us look at Example 4—Primitive Pythagorean Triples. One observation was:

4. x and y seem to have different parity.

A question following this observation might be, "Can you find a primitive Pythagorean triple in which this is *not* the case?" This question is generated by an *observation;* other questions are generated by *conjectures*—perhaps based on apparent regularity or predictability, coupled with the desire to find out if that appearance is realized. Especially with regard to data, but applicable in other areas as well, a helpful heuristic for seeing things in new ways would be to separate out

1. the making of observations
2. the asking of questions, and
3. the coming up with conjectures.

It is the eventual intertwining of these three activities that creates the force that enables us to see beyond "a glass darkly."

One strategy then for phase-one problem generation involves an attempt to focus upon observations, conjectures and questions without being concerned with interrelating them at first. Eventually, however, we attempt to do so.

Internal Versus External Exploration

It is perhaps a legacy of our technological society that when we see something new, we are more inclined to ask how its parts fit together than how it (taken as a whole in some vague way) might relate to other phenomena. To look at an automobile *internally* is to ask questions about how its parts fit together. To ask questions about it externally, however, is to suggest not only that we explore how one automobile relates to others, but how the automobile as a class relates to other means of transportation or other phenomena like the quality of life in society.[4]

Notice that in the beginning of our exploration of the isosceles triangle in Example 2, we questioned internal workings. We assumed that the object of our concern was how the pieces of one isosceles triangle interacted with each other in isolation from other triangles. We asked, for example, about the symmetry of the triangle. We did not consider taking the triangle as a single object to be related to other such triangles until we asked the question: What figures can you make with two or even three or more congruent isosceles triangles? (Question 6).

Looking back at this question, we notice that it frees us from the restriction of looking only at *internal* workings—a restriction we often impose on ourselves without realizing it. Appreciating that we have explored one external type of question enables us to search for others. In the Supreme Court case, for example, we might ask what the consequences would be if three members of the legislature

---

[4]This distinction is elaborated in the context of analyzing "understanding" by Jane Martin, *Explaining, Understanding and Teaching,* New York, McGraw-Hill, 1970, pp. 152–163.

were to join the nine judges and the judges were expected to greet the members of the legislature by handshaking.

Such external type of investigation was done in the case of the isosceles triangle example when, instead of exploring the workings of one such triangle, we combined triangles as described above. Further external investigation might lead us to relate the isosceles triangle to other figures—to determine perhaps, how they might be combined with each other in the creation of patterns. We could even move beyond the relationship of such patterns in mathematics and include domains of inquiry such as art, architecture and other areas as well.

Exact Versus Approximate Explorations

An important strategy for exploring a problem stems from the notion that we need not necessarily aim for exact answers. Notice that in the Supreme Court example, a number of questions were directed at efforts to approximate answers, even before exact calculations were suggested. It is extremely important mathematically as well as intellectually to appreciate that there are times not only when it is unnecessary and undesirable to get exact answers, but when it is impossible to do so. It would be worthwhile to take a look once more at many of the questions we have posed in this section to determine what would be lost by searching not for an exact answer, but an approximation instead. Take some of these questions and try to modify them, so that they are transformed from a request for a precise response to one for an approximate response. You might try to relate this activity both to any other mathematical activity you may be involved with, and to your non-mathematical life as well. How much is lost by searching for a less exact analysis or a less precise strategy?

Historical Exploration: Actual versus Hypothetical

In this section, we will suggest how it is possible to generate significant questions by making use of historical ways of thinking, despite the fact that you may not be a historian and may, in fact, know very little about the history of the idea or phenomenon under investigation.

In the case of isosceles triangle, we asked the question: What was it that encouraged people initially to investigate isosceles triangles? (Question 5). An exploration of this question would involve the study of history—something which requires an expertise that few of us have. It is possible, however, to slightly modify these questions so we need not be historians. We could let our imaginations have free reign and consider what *might have been* the historical antecedents. For example, we could ask:

What *might have* encouraged people to investigate isosceles triangles?
or

What *might have* accounted for people's interest in the Pythagorean relation?

With regard to the first question, one reasonable answer might be that it was merely an effort at classification. Another might be that a special kind of triangle enabled people to get a handle on conjectures that were hard to prove in general. The importance of asking and searching for answers to these questions is that such inquiry forces us not merely to prove things, but rather to locate the *significance* of a topic we are asked to investigate. The importance of this issue is raised in an anecdote of Edwin Moise. He comments:

> A distinguished algebraist once served as an examiner in a final oral for the doctorate, based on a dissertation on Banach algebras. Toward the end of the examination, the algebraist asked the student to describe some examples of Banach algebras. The student was able . . . to name one example, but his one example was trivial.[5]

As Moise points out, though the dissertation director could have justified the student's research, the student—who had solved a number of mathematical problems—had no good intellectual reason for working on those problems in the first place.

Yet all of us know good problem solvers who do not necessarily appreciate the significance of the activity in which they are engaged. We recall our experience with Jordan, a bright young man who was confused by what the ambiguous case in trigonometry was all about. Trying to put the issue in perspective, he was reminded of his prior geometry course in which he had investigated those conditions under which a triangle was determined (S.A.S., A.S.A., S.S.S., or A.S.S.—which is the ambiguous case). He was confused for a while and finally complained, "What do you mean? We never studied how a triangle is determined. We only did things like prove that two triangles were congruent if S.A.S. = S.A.S." Here is a beautiful example of an honor student who could prove a great deal, but had little appreciation for why it was significant for him to prove these things.

To look at the significance of something, then, is not only to prove things or to investigate them more generally, but to try to figure out why they are worth investigating in the first place. While we would all be hard pressed to explore everything we engage in from the perspective of whether or not and why it may be significant, we certainly do see things differently when we ask questions of that sort. Pseudo-history thus becomes one more tool that we can use to generate a set of questions that enable us to search for significance.

---

[5]Edwin Moise, "Activity and Motivation in Mathematics," *American Mathematical Monthly,* April, 1965, p. 410.

A Handy List of Questions

If we look back at some of the questions we have asked in this chapter and incorporate others that we and our students have used in much of our mathematical explorations, we arrive at a list of general questions that could provide yet one more point of departure for problem generation even at this early stage. These questions do not apply to specific content; instead they are a master list. Though some of these questions might be incorporated into some of our other problem posing strategies, they are nevertheless valuable as an independent starting point of their own. We list a number of these starting questions with the understanding that they will provide a handy point of departure for you. This list is not complete, of course, and never can be. As you go through this book, you will want to add other questions of your own. It will be interesting, at various points in your reading, to look back at the expanded list to see which kinds of questions you tend to favor. Perhaps you might enjoy comparing your favorites with those of a colleague.

Here is a beginning list generated in one of our classes.

A List of Questions

Is there a formula?

What is the formula?

What purpose does the formula serve?

What is the number of objects or cases satisfying this condition?

What is the maximum?

What is the minimum?

What is the range of the answer?

Is there a pattern here?

What is the pattern in this case?

Is there a counterexample?

Can it be extended?

Does it exist?

Is there a solution?

Can we find the solution?

How can we condense the information?

Can we make a table?

Can we prove it?

When is it false? When true?

Is it constant?

What is constant; what is variable?

Does it depend on something we can specify?

Is there a limiting case?

What is the domain?

Where does the proof break down in an analogous situation?

Is there a uniting theme?

Is it relevant?

Are we imposing an restrictions without intending to do so?

When is it relevant?

What does it remind you of?

How can one salvage what appears to be a breakdown?

How can you view it geometrically?

How can you view it algebraically?

How can you view it analytically?

What do they have in common?

What do I need in order to prove this?

What are key features of the situation?

What are the key constraints currently being imposed on the situation?

Does viewing actual data suggest anything interesting?

How does this relate to other things?

A word of caution is necessary for anyone using our list (yours, or anyone else's) or trying to teach problem posing and solving with it. It is necessary to understand the special circumstances of a situation which might make it appropriate to use preconceived lenses to illuminate that situation. It might be foolish to apply some of these questions in certain circumstances. On the other hand, we should be equally aware that a nonsensical-sounding question might apply if we were willing to modify what might be our own rigid mind set.

Mathematics itself is studded with examples of questions that appeared to be foolish or inapplicable due to a vision that was limited. A question like, "If we take the side of a square to have unit length, how many times longer is the diagonal than its side?" was essentially a non-question for those unable to associate the diagonal of a square with a number. The question, "How can I show that Euclid's fifth postulate does *not* follow from his others?" was not asked for over 2,000 years because people were so committed to it being an inconceivable possibility. Even when we are convinced that a question, such as, "Which is more prime: 181 or 191?" is meaningless (which we should be cautious to do), frequently a slight modification of the question will bring it into line.

While we are not suggesting that every nonsensical question eventually incorporated (perhaps modified) in a given situation will guarantee historic posterity, it is possible that some worthwhile insight could follow. The next chapter will demonstrate how such questions can be the catalyst for valuable reflection even for topics in a standard curriculum.

4

The Second Phase of Problem Posing: "What-If-Not"

SEEING WHAT IS IN FRONT OF YOU

Do we always "see" what is in front of us? The most obvious things are frequently those most hidden from us. Sometimes it takes a bit of a rude awakening for us to appreciate what is right before us and, often, some kind of reorganization or shift of perspective leads us to see the obvious. For instance, a personal disaster may have the ironic effect of enabling us to see love, friendship, and blessings that may not have been perceived beforehand.

You most likely have had experience in problem solving that illustrates this point. On a perceptual level, you might take the drawing in Figure 2 as an example.

What is it a picture of? Most people will say that it is six equilateral triangles

---

"Sherman on the Mount" reprinted by permission of artist.

FIG. 2.

or a hexagon with the diagonals drawn in. Very few people will see it as a drawing of something three-dimensional, although occasionally a few people see it as the top of a tent. Sometimes the suggestion that it might be three-dimensional is enough to trigger an "ah-ha" response, as the person shifts perspective to see it as a cube. Of course, there are many additional ways of interpreting this drawing.

On a more cognitive level, perhaps one of the most famous of the "ah-ha" solutions was Gauss's recognition that

$$1 + 2 + 3 + \ldots + 97 + 98 + 99 + 100$$

can be calculated easily by noticing that we can consider the series as many pairs of numbers summing to 101.

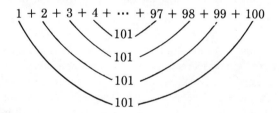

The shift of visual and cognitive perspectives may appear so obvious once we achieve it, that we may not appreciate that the task was a non-trivial one.

It is one thing to appreciate something from a fresh point of view; it is another to show that such a fresh point of view can be productive. For example, $x^2 - x + 41$ is often given as a formula that generates only prime numbers for different values of x. One sometimes teases students into believing it might be true in general by substituting x = 1, 2, 3. Often people continue substituting successive values of x, thus strengthening their belief that the formula generates only prime numbers. Those who shift their perspective by asking, "For what value of x does the formula break down?" come to see the limitations of the formula faster than those who attempt to search for positive evidence. It breaks down at x = 41, a fact that requires virtually no calculation but merely the observation that for x = 41, we are left with 41^2 which is obviously not a prime. Of course a change in perspective is not always accompanied by an "ah-ha" experience (though it frequently is) nor need it be productive.

It is ironic that it is so difficult for us to see what supposedly stares us in the face, since so much of mathematical thinking begins with the assumption that we take the "given" for granted. We are trained to begin a proof by first stating and accepting what is given. If we are asked to prove in a right triangle, with right angle at C, that $c^2 = a^2 + b^2$, we begin by assuming that we have a right triangle with sides a, b, c, and for this kind of proof, a clear statement of the given is a necessary first step.

But all of this training hides several very important points about mathematical thinking. First of all, in most contexts (except those that have been contrived in classrooms) it is not so easy to see what is given. What we decide to take as given depends on our purposes, available intellectual tools, aesthetic desires, and so forth. For example, many of you are familiar with the fact that it is impossible in general to trisect an angle—one of three well known classical problems of antiquity. The proof of the impossibility of trisection, depends in some not so obvious ways upon "the given" that construction is to be done with a straight edge and a pair of compasses. If we assume an implement known as a tomahawk however, it is easy to prove that it is possible to trisect any angle.[1] It is a fascinating issue to locate where in the proof using a tomahawk we violate the assumptions of the Euclidean instruments. It is also worth thinking about why Euclidean tools were considered sacred.

Secondly, taking the given for granted usually assumes that our job is one of *proving something* based on the given. But there is certainly much more to mathematics than proving things. Coming up with a new idea, finding an appropriate image to enable us to hold on to an old one, evaluating the significance of an idea we have already learned, or seeing new connections are also reasonable mathematical activities. For these and many other activities, we need a different notion than that of merely specifying and accepting the given as it is used in problem solving.

ATTRIBUTE LISTING FOR A NEW PROBLEM POSING STRATEGY

How can we go beyond accepting the given? First we try to specify what we see as "the given," though as we indicated earlier this is sometimes more difficult to do than we would imagine. Let us illustrate what we mean, first by using a theorem, and then by using a concrete material.

Using A Theorem

Let us go back to the Pythagorean theorem as an illustration. What is given? As suggested in the previous section, we are asking for many different possible

---

[1]See Howard Eves *An Introduction to the History of Mathematics,* Holt, Rinehart and Winston, New York, third edition, 1969, pp. 84–87.

interpretations of what is in front of us. How would you describe the Pythagorean theorem?

The following is a list of some of the responses to the question that we have received.

1. The statement is a theorem.
2. The theorem deals with lengths of line segments.
3. The theorem deals with right triangles.
4. The theorem deals with areas.
5. The theorem deals with squares.
6. There are three variables associated with the Pythagorean theorem.
7. The variables are related by an equals sign.
8. There is a plus sign between two of the variables.
9. There are three exponents all of which are the same.
10. The exponents are positive integers.

We can call the ten preceding statements some attributes of the theorem. In what ways do the first five statements differ from the other five? At first glance, it seems as if the first five resulted from viewing the theorem geometrically, while the last five statements viewed it algebraically. However, we realize that more is involved because in some cases we deal with the *logic* of the statement, while in others we focus on the *substance* of the statement.

These kinds of distinctions point out that there are many ways of seeing the given. Regardless of these distinctions, what have we done so far? We have chosen an example—a theorem, the Pythagorean theorem—and we have made a list of some of its attributes. Different people will obviously produce different lists. Note that the list of attributes can never be complete and that the attributes need not be independent of each other. That is, we might have listed as attributes the fact that the theorem has a long and interesting history or the triangle has a right angle and the fact that the two acute angles add up to 90°. We call the listing of attributes Level I of our scheme, and the branches of Figure 3 indicate a few of the attributes.

We can depict schematically in Figure 3 what we have done so far.

This is just the beginning of our scheme. Before continuing, let us demonstrate further what we mean by attributes by choosing a second, different type of starting point: A concrete material instead of an abstract theorem.

Concrete Material: Geoboards

We now return to the concrete material which we introduced in chapter 3, the geoboard, to develop the scheme suggested in Figure 3.

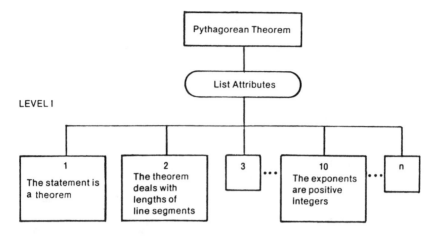

FIG. 3.

Now, study the geoboard in Figure 4. How would you describe it?

Some people might say that there are twenty-five nails arranged in a square array; others might mention that the board is white. Various attributes we have heard mentioned include:

1. The board is square.
2. The markings are regularly spaced.
3. The markings are spaced along square lattice points.
4. The markings are nails.
5. The additional objects are rubber bands.
6. The board is 5 × 5—that is, it has twenty-five nails on it.
7. The board is rigid.
8. The markings on this board are only on one side of the board.
9. The nails are all of the same height.
10. The board is stationary (unless picked up and moved).
11. The board is simply connected.

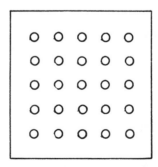

FIG. 4.

You might well be thinking that attribute 10 is silly or that attribute 4 is irrelevant. However, we will soon see that apparently silly or irrelevant attributes may lead to worthwhile investigation. The question of which attributes are significant is not always easy to answer beforehand, and furthermore it is difficult to make such a judgment unless you have some idea of the purpose of the board. For example, we would expect the yoga expert to answer this question differently from the mathematician. Similarly, we shall not consider the whiteness of the board to be a significant variable. The fact that the board is all the same color (or the color could be varied within a given geoboard) might be significant even from a mathematical point of view to someone who is deeply interested in topological problems (such as the famous four color problem). In any case, it is better to put an attribute in that might not be useful than to leave it out. In short, when in doubt, leave it in!

You may wish at this point to draw a schematic diagram for the geoboard which is analogous to the one we drew for the Pythagorean theorem (Figure 3). You might now be asking, "Where does this Level I attribute listing lead?" To show the value of it, let us continue with the geoboard. Later we will apply our techniques to the Pythagorean theorem.

NOW WHAT? A LOOK AT THREE ATTRIBUTES OF GEOBOARDS

As soon as we look at the geoboard as an object whose attributes are variable and not as an unchangeable object, a host of new possibilities emerges.

The first attribute we might vary is squareness. In order to generate new ideas about the geoboard, we ask ourselves, "What if the board were not square? What could it be?" Let us allow our imaginations free reign. Instead of square we might think of boards that are:

circular   triangular

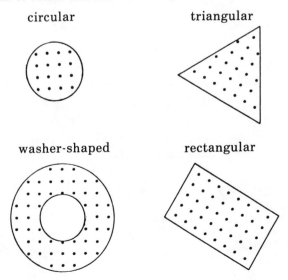

washer-shaped   rectangular

Notice that in all the shapes generated so far, we have employed a hidden assumption: flatness. This suggests that flatness may be another attribute to vary and it is not one we listed before. We may also notice that all the shapes are finite and bounded. While squareness and flatness may be immediately obvious attributes of the board, the latter two attributes are less apparent and, as a matter of fact, became obvious to us only after we attempted to vary squareness and flatness. Thus, not only does looking for a new variation of an attribute suggest new geoboards, but it suggests additional attributes of the standard one as well.

An Alternative to Squareness: Circularity

Consider a circular geoboard. Let us change only the shape of the board and not the spacing of the nails. In asking how this board differs from the square geoboard, we realize that it is essentially a square geoboard with certain nails removed. This leads us to consider the question, "How many nails would be eliminated if we were to cut the largest circular board out of a square one?"[2] Clearly, for a 2 × 2 board all 4 nails would be eliminated to form a circle. We are assuming here that the geoboard has no border beyond that determined by its outermost set of nails (Figure 5[a]).

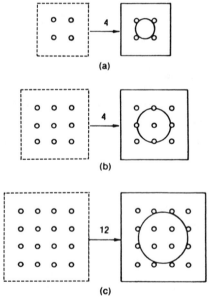

(a)

(b)

(c)

FIG. 5.

[2]We are assuming that our theoretical square geoboard has no border beyond the square grid of nails, and hence for the first board all 4 nails would have to be removed in cutting out the largest possible circular board.

For a 3 × 3 geoboard (Figure 5[b]), four of the nine nails disappear. For a 4 × 4 board (Figure 5[c]), twelve nails are removed. You might want to try the problem for a 5 × 5 board. We summarize our exploration in Table 2.

TABLE 2
The Largest Circular Geoboard Cut From A Square Geoboard

Size of Square Board	Number of Nails on Square Board	Number of Nails Eliminated	Number of Nails on Circular Board
1 × 1	1	0	0
2 × 2	4	4	0
3 × 3	9	4	5
4 × 4	16	12	4
5 × 5	25	12	13
6 × 6	36	20	16
7 × 7	49	20	29
8 × 8	64	32	32
9 × 9	81	32	49

It would be worthwhile (partly because the answer is not apparent) for you to predict the number of nails which would remain on an n × n geoboard that is cut into the largest possible circle. Though this problem has been generated within the context of a new kind of geoboard, it is worth realizing that this same question can be analyzed in the case of a standard geoboard. For example, instead of rubber bands as an adjunct of the standard geoboard, we could use wire circles and ask, "What is the maximum number of nails that can be enclosed by a wire circle on the board?"

Now let us turn to another variation of the geoboard. We start by challenging the attribute that the markings are placed along square lattice points.

An Alternative to Square Lattice Points: Shearing

Suppose the nails are not placed as a square lattice but at vertices of a grid such as the sheared one shown in Figure 6.

Do new questions suggest themselves to you, now that we are looking at a different board? Do any of the new questions have meaning for the old board? For which questions will the answers be the same for the square lattice as well as for the sheared one?

Let us compare the two boards by looking at one example in more detail. We can think of our geoboard as graph paper and consider the two edges as our axes. Suppose we label the axes in both cases □ and △. In addition, we have drawn in two lines. Notice that the pairs of lines are analogously placed in each diagram.

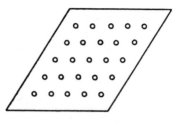

FIG. 6.

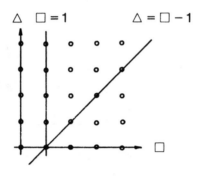

FIG. 7.

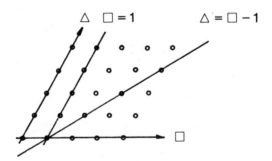

FIG. 8.   (Compare with Figure 7)

In what ways can we compare these two lines in the two diagrams?[3] We could ask, "How do the equations of these lines compare? How do their points of intersection compare?" In what other ways could we compare the boards?

_____

[3]As we start we might ask: Why did we see the two new lines in figure 8 as analogously placed in relationship to those in Figure 7?

We might consider regions, for instance. Now, draw any polygonal region on the square lattice board. Now imagine that you have sheared the square lattice board. Now draw this new shape on the sheared board. Choosing a square as a unit for the square board, decide how you would analogously define a unit of area on the sheared board. What is the area of the new sheared figure and how does it compare with the old one?

In the two examples just given we have, in effect, asked whether or not a rearrangement of lattice points alters the answer to the questions we pose. Can it make the original question meaningless? Here we can even ask a question which arises out of a direct comparison of the two boards and which goes beyond analogy. For example, if you place the square geoboard in Figure 7 on top of the sheared geoboard in Figure 8 so that the bottom row of nails coincides, will any other nails coincide? Does the answer depend on the angle of shear? (Assume here that the same unit of length is chosen along axes for Figures 7 and 8).

To continue to see how exploring alternatives to an attribute can lead to new ideas, we shall consider in some detail one other attribute of the standard geoboard—that of finiteness.

An Alternative to Finiteness: Infinite Boards

What kinds of phenomena are suggested when we consider finiteness as a variable, while maintaining most of the other attributes of the geoboard? The board can obviously be infinite (and also unbounded) in a number of essentially different ways, though no physical model of it can exist. What would be your first reaction to drawing an infinite geoboard?

Figure 9 shows some different ways in which the board might be made infinite in extent.

Figures 9(a), (b) and (c) respectively depict half plane, full plane and quarter plane infinite lattices. In Figure 9(d), we vary the quarter plane lattice by changing the number of degrees in the angle between the axes. There are, of course, other kinds of variations which lead to an infinite array.

Let us focus here on one model, Figure 9(c). One fanciful way of interpreting it is as an infinite orchard with trees equally spaced.[4] Let each dot represent a tree (with no thickness, of course). Suppose a person is sitting at the origin. Let us suppose further that one sees along straight line paths from the origin, and that any tree along a line of vision blocks trees behind it (on the same line of vision). There are a number of questions which relate to this phenomenon. For example:

---

[4]Though it was not conceived of as a variation to the geoboard, the notion of such an orchard is discussed by Martin Gardner, "Mathematical Games," *Scientific American,* May 1965, pp. 120–126. We will pose a number of questions here which were not suggested therein.

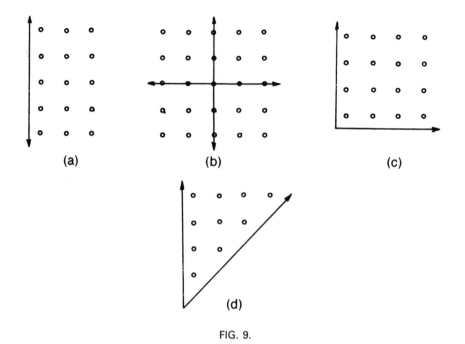

FIG. 9.

1. Given a tree in the lattice, is it visible or blocked?
2. Does every line of vision hit a tree somewhere (perhaps far off) on the lattice?
3. Can the person at the origin systematically number the trees (1, 2, 3, . . .) so that given any number no matter how large, he can tell where in the orchard the tree associated with that number is located?
4. Suppose the man is placed on a rotating wheel chair at the origin and he is spun in a random fashion within lines of vision of the quarter plane. What is the probability that when his chair stops, his line of vision will have no trees along it?

The fact that some people's response to Question 2 would most likely be yes, suggests that they are in for quite a shock when they learn that the answer to Question 4 ("What is the probability that when the chair stops, the line of vision will have no tree along it?") is one.[5] You can think of additional questions that

---

[5]In order to appreciate that there is at least one line of vision not blocked by a tree (question 2 above), consider the line defined by the equation $y = \sqrt{2} \cdot x$. Finding integral values for x and y would be tantamount to expressing $\sqrt{2}$ as a rational number—something that is impossible. Once we have nailed down one such line of vision by use of an irrational slope, it is possible to imagine an infinite number of such lines. The probability of 1 is a consequence of the uncountability of the irrational numbers in relationship to the rational numbers, a concept that is far from intuitively obvious, but beyond the scope of this discussion.

involve many other areas. You might, for example, wish to reconsider questions of this sort once we allow for thickness of the trees. Also, what new questions are suggested, and how are answers to the previous ones modified if the person in the quarter plane is no longer seated at the origin?

WHAT HAVE WE DONE?

Look at Figure 3 once more. Recall that previously we chose a theorem and then listed the attributes. This time we selected a concrete material, the geoboard, and looking at the geoboard, we listed attributes. There were many of them (such as the board is square, the board is finite . . .). We thought of many of the attributes at the start, while others occurred to us only later. We depict what we have done with attribute listing on the geoboard in Figure 10. (You might find it useful to compare it to the scheme depicted in Figure 3.) In Figure 10 we indicate that we do not know how many attributes we will eventually list by drawing branches up to the nth one.

But notice we have in fact done more than this chart would imply. Not only have we asked, "What are some attributes?" but we have also asked, "What are some alternatives to any given attribute?" We have also asked additional questions concerning the new attributes.

So after listing some attributes of the geoboard which we call Level I, we asked for each attribute "What-If-Not?" that attribute. For example, for Attribute 1, "The board is square" led us to ask, "What if the board were not square?" We call this "What-If-Not?" question asking Level II(a). What other shape could the board be? Some answers were that the board is circular, or

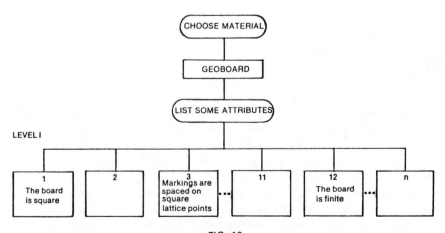

FIG. 10.

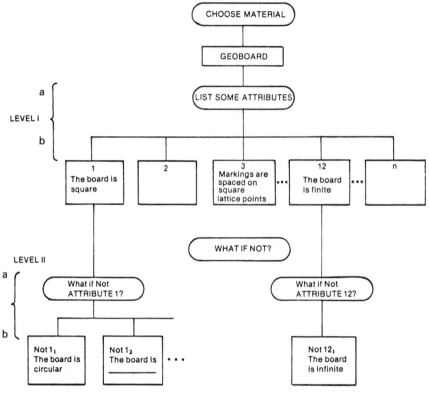

FIG. 11.

triangular. We call these answers Level II(b). We depict these first two levels of our scheme in Figure 11. It was in this way that we were led to consider:

- a circular geoboard
- the sheared arrangement of nails
- an "infinite" array of nails

Notice that in Level II of Figure 11 we have only indicated *one* "What-If-Not" for each of the two attributes. Under squareness, for example, we listed only one alternative—circularity. Of course we could have considered any other alternative to squareness (such as rectangular shaped or washer shaped) and pursued it in depth too.

But what does it mean to pursue something in depth in this context? *It means to ask a question about it as a start.* Notice in the case of the circular geoboard we asked only one question, while in the case of an infinite board we asked many. You may wish to return to the circular board and ask further questions. In order to generate questions, we can make use of all of the strategies for question asking that we indicated in chapter 3. This step of question asking which comes after listing attributes and asking "What-If-Not" for any particular attribute, is the next step in our scheme and we call it Level III. So far, then, we have demonstrated three levels in our scheme: Level I (list attributes), Level II (ask for each one, "What if it were not so?") and finally Level III (pose questions).

In Figure 11, we have simplified the process by listing only a few attributes and by suggesting one alternative for each of two attributes. In Figure 12, we have indicated the asking of questions (Level III). You might wish to sketch just the branches for one attribute, two alternatives and two new questions on these alternatives! Of course we have provided the diagram only to help explain our scheme; when actually using the scheme, there is no need to draw a diagram.

A RETURN TO THE PYTHAGOREAN THEOREM

"What-If-Not" on Some Attributes

Now that we have the first few stages of our problem posing scheme, let us reconsider the Pythagorean theorem. Look again at our list of the attributes of the Pythagorean theorem (Level I of our scheme). How can we use this list of attributes to help us pose new problems? We can use the same strategies as we just did for the geoboard and follow through the same steps.

Beginning the "What-If-Not" Strategy

What did we do in the case of the geoboard after we listed attributes? We took an attribute and asked "What-If-Not" that attribute. We will do the same for the attributes of the Pythagorean theorem. We will illustrate this second step (Level II) by using several attributes as an example.

Attribute 1. The statement is a *theorem*. How else could we construe the statement? i.e., What if it were not a theorem? What could it be?

Just to *ask* such a question is in many cases a bold move—one that takes courage! Great advances in knowledge have taken place by people who have had the courage to look at a cluster of attributes and to ask, "What-If-Not?" As we mentioned earlier, perhaps the most famous such instance in mathematics involves the development of non-Euclidean geometry. Up through the 18th century, mathematicians had tried in vain to prove the parallel postulate as a theorem. It took 2,000 years before mathematicians were prepared to even ask the question, "*What if it were not* the case that through a given external point there was exactly one line parallel to a given line? What if there were at least two? None? What would that do to the structure of geometry?"

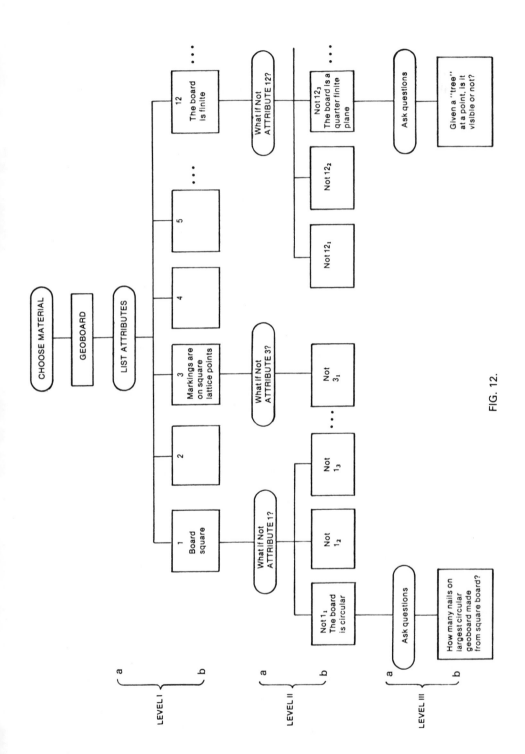

FIG. 12.

44

Cantor's work on countability (alluded to earlier in the infinite orchard) is another example of the intellectual leaps someone can make by questioning "obvious" givens. Great advances in modern science from Harvey (What if it were not the case that a great quantity of blood was constantly produced and dissipated into the body cavity?) to Einstein (What if time and space were not absolute, independent entities?) have depended in part on "What-If-Not" formulations of a problem. Some people have even been burned at the stake or have taken hemlock for "What-If-Not" formulations of an idea!

Return to Attribute 1: The statement is a theorem. How could one answer "What-If-Not" in this case? Let us symbolize alternatives by (~ 1), which means "not attribute 1."[6] Let us label the various alternatives by subscripts such as $(\sim 1)_2$.

$(\sim 1)_1$ Construe the statement as a definition.

$(\sim 1)_2$ Construe the statement as an axiom.

$(\sim 1)_3$ Assume the statement is false, i.e., $a^2 + b^2 \neq c^2$ (as, for example, in non-Euclidean geometry).

Does it seem far-fetched to construe the Pythagorean theorem as an axiom? Some people have pursued the consequences of choosing the theorem as an axiom. Even just listing this alternative increases our awareness of the statement as a theorem.

Before picking an alternative to examine carefully, let us continue to increase our options by listing "What-If-Not" alternatives for the other attributes of the Pythagorean theorem.

Attribute 2.   The theorem deals with lengths of the three sides. What if it did not deal with lengths of the sides? Focusing on length, we might choose the following formulations for "What-If-Not" Attribute 2.

$(\sim 2)_1$ Consider half-lengths of the sides.

$(\sim 2)_2$ Look at various projections of the three sides.

$(\sim 2)_3$ Look at the orientation of the three sides.

Attribute 3.   The theorem deals with a right triangle. What if the theorem did not deal with right triangles? What else could it be?

$(\sim 3)_1$ Consider an acute triangle.

$(\sim 3)_2$ Consider an obtuse triangle.

---

[6]In this case the negation becomes " 'not' the statement is a theorem" which in better English might read "the statement is not a theorem."

Although it may seem absurd at first, let us not rule out listing the following cases because they might prove fruitful:

$(\sim 3)_3$ A straight angle "triangle."

$(\sim 3)_4$ A reflex "triangle."

$(\sim 3)_5$ Consider a right four-sided figure (notice here we re-focused our attention from "right" to "triangle").

Attribute 4. The theorem deals with areas.

$(\sim 4)_1$ Suppose it deals with volume.

$(\sim 4)_2$ Consider higher (or lower) dimensions.

Attribute 5. The theorem deals with squares.

$(\sim 5)_1$ Consider rectangles on the sides.

$(\sim 5)_2$ Consider triangles on the sides.

$(\sim 5)_3$ Consider similar polygons (non-polygons) on the sides.

$(\sim 5)_4$ Consider random polygons on the sides.

Attribute 6. There are three variables associated with the Pythagorean theorem. What if there were not three variables? What could be the case then? Among possibilities might be:

$(\sim 6)_1$ Suppose there were four variables. For example, $a^2 + b^2 = d^2 + c^2$ or $a^2 + b^2 + c^2 = d^2$.

$(\sim 6)_2$ Suppose there were two variables, for example $a^2 = b^2$.

$(\sim 6)_3$ Suppose there were three variables and some constants; for example,
$$a^2 + b^2 = c^2 + n.$$

$(\sim 6)_4$ Suppose there were two variables and a constant; for example,
$$a^2 + b^2 = n.$$

Attribute 7. The variables are related by an "equals sign." What if this were not the case? What could the relationship be? Some possibilities are:

$(\sim 7)_1$ The variables are related by "$<$": $a^2 + b^2 < c^2$.

$(\sim 7)_2$ The variables are related by "$\leq$": $a^2 + b^2 \leq c^2$.

$(\sim 7)_3$ The variables are related by division: $a^2 + b^2$ divides c^2.

$(\sim 7)_4$ The variables are related by "$>$": $a^2 + b^2 > c^2$.

$(\sim 7)_5$ $a^2 + b^2$ and c^2 are relatively prime.

$(\sim 7)_6$ $a^2 + b^2$ differs from c^2 by a constant.

Attribute 8.   There is a plus sign between two of the variables.

$(\sim 8)_1$ $a^2 - b^2 = c^2$.
$(\sim 8)_2$ $a^2 \cdot b^2 = c^2$.
$(\sim 8)_3$ $(a^2)^{b^2} = c^2$.
$(\sim 8)_4$ $a^2 \div b^2 = c^2$.

Attribute 9.   There are three exponents, all of which are the same. Some "What-If-Nots":

$(\sim 9)_1$ $a + b^2 = c^2$.
$(\sim 9)_2$ $a + b = c^2$.
$(\sim 9)_3$ $a^2 + b^3 = c^5$.
$(\sim 9)_4$ $a^2 + b^2 = c$.

Attribute 10.   The exponents are positive integers. Some

$(\sim 10)_1$ $a^{1/2} + b^{1/2} = c^{1/2}$.
$(\sim 10)_2$ $a^{-1} + b^{-1} = c^{-1}$.
$(\sim 10)_3$ $a^{\sqrt{2}} + b^{\sqrt{2}} = c^{\sqrt{2}}$.

Now we have taken ten attributes of the Pythagorean theorem and have generated two or more alternatives for each. For Attribute 7, we generated six alternatives and altogether we have generated over thirty alternatives. What do we do with this list of "What-If-Not" alternatives? This list is made useful as we progress to our Level III activity, that of asking a question. Let us demonstrate this third level by looking at Attribute 7 as a start.

Brainstorming on One Changed Attribute

Asking a Question

As we have shown, there are many possible variations of Attribute 7. Let us choose one of them to demonstrate how alternatives to attributes can give rise to new investigations.

Consider $(\sim 7)_1$: The variables are related by a "$<$" sign: $a^2 + b^2 < c^2$. What questions come to mind? Several possibilities are:

$(\sim 7)_1$ (a):   Does $a^2 + b^2 < c^2$ have any geometrical significance?
$(\sim 7)_1$ (b):   For what numbers is the inequality $a^2 + b^2 < c^2$ true?
$(\sim 7)_1$ (c):   How many instances are there for which $a^2 + b^2$ differs from c^2 by a particular constant? (i.e., $a^2 + b^2 = k + c^2$ for a fixed k).
$(\sim 7)_1$ (d):   What is the graph of $a^2 + b^2 < c^2$?

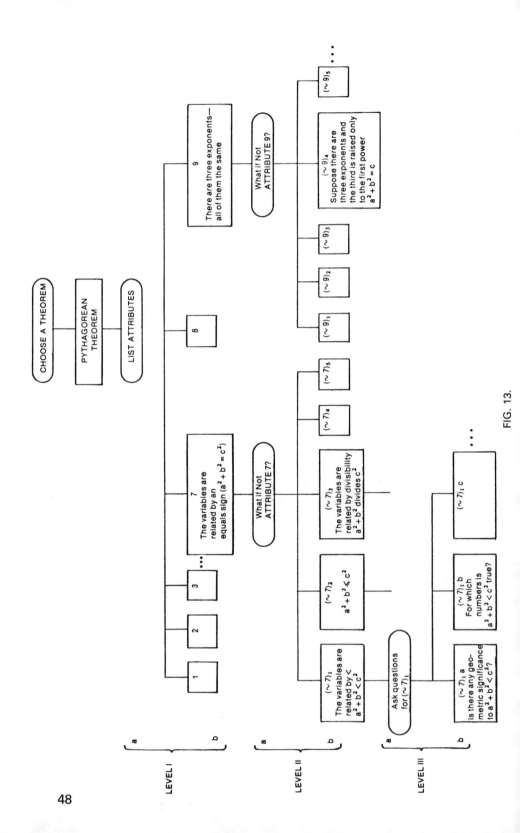

FIG. 13.

48

Let us stress again that we have done more than merely listing attributes (Level I of our scheme) and modifying attributes by asking "What-If-Not"? (Level II). We have just posed some new questions (Level III). We would probably not have thought of these questions without having gone through Level I and Level II. For the purpose of brainstorming ideas, proposing "What-If-Not" is only Level II and must be followed by question asking.

In Figure 13 for example, we have shown two attributes, Attributes 7 and 9. Attribute 7 is, "The variables are related by an equals sign $a^2 + b^2 = c^2$" and three alternatives to this attribute are given. They are:

$(\sim 7)_1$ The variables are related by $<$, $a^2 + b^2 < c^3$.

$(\sim 7)_2$ The variables are related by $\leq$, $a^2 + b^2 \leq c^2$.

$(\sim 7)_3$ The variables are related by divisibility, $a^2 + b^2$ divides c^2.

Attribute 9 is, "There are three exponents—all of them the same." One alternative to Attribute 9 is shown in the diagram (namely, that there are three exponents of which the third is raised only to the first power). But in both cases—Attribute 7 and Attribute 9—it is not until we ask a question that there is the potential for gaining anything new. We urge you to trace through other branches of the diagram, making your own choices of attributes and "What-If-Not" alternatives and questions.

Posing new questions is a valuable activity. Let us demonstrate this by indicating how a newly posed question may help us gain some deeper insight into the nature of the Pythagorean relationship which was our starting point.

Analyzing a Question

Let us take two of the questions we posed and see how analyzing and trying to answer them gives us a deeper insight into the Pythagorean theorem. So often people have a feeling that once they "know" a theorem they know all there is to it! So let us look at two of the questions we posed after we wrote down a "What-If-Not" to Attribute 7, namely $a^2 + b^2 < c^2$. The first question posed was, "Does $a^2 + b^2 < c^2$ have any geometric significance?"

The second question posed was, "For what whole numbers does this inequality hold?" You may wish to defer the details of the analysis of the first questions to a second reading.

Your first step might be to translate the algebraic inequality into the geometrical assertion: The sum of the squares on the two legs of a right triangle is less than the square on the hypotenuse. Though we know from the Pythagorean theorem that this is never the case for a right triangle with right angle at C, under what circumstances might it be true?

Suppose we relax the criterion that the triangle be at a right triangle but maintain our focus, using conventional notations that c is the side opposite angle C. Under what conditions can $a^2 + b^2$ be less than c^2 and what is the geometric significance?

The law of cosines asserts that for any three sides a, b and c of a triangle, $a^2 + b^2 = c^2 + 2ab \cos C$. Therefore $a^2 + b^2 < c^2$ whenever $2ab \cos C$ is negative. This occurs only when angle C is obtuse, as in the picture below.

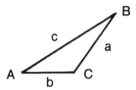

Since the question ("Under what conditions is $a^2 + b^2 < c^2$?") is understandable to one who knows nothing about trigonometry, it is interesting to note that the problem is also *analyzable* without the law of cosines. If $a^2 + b^2 < c^2$, then c must be larger than what it would be if angle C were a right angle. Hence ∡ C must be obtuse. We might also ask if we could somehow appreciate the geometric significance of $c^2 - (a^2 + b^2)$, the amount by which $a^2 + b^2$ falls short of c^2.

Let us recall the drawing used by Euclid in his proof of the Pythagorean theorem. See Figure 14. He proved the theorem by showing that the square on $\overline{BC}$ has the same area as rectangle BKME [Figure 14(a)] and that the square on $\overline{CA}$ has the same area as the rectangle KADM [Figure 14(b)]. Thus the square on $\overline{BC}$ plus the square on $\overline{AC}$ equals the square on $\overline{AB}$.

Now let us look at what happens when ∡C is not a right angle. Since $\overline{AB}$ is shorter (longer) if ∡C is acute (obtuse), the square on $\overline{AB}$ cannot now be equal to the square on $\overline{BC}$ plus the square on $\overline{AC}$. The difference between the area of the square on AB and the sum of the squares on the other two sides of the triangle is called the defect. If ∡C is obtuse, then the area of the square on $\overline{AB}$ is larger than the sum of the other two areas, while if ∡C is acute the area of the square on $\overline{AB}$ is smaller. See Figure 15. Let us take the case in which ∡C measures more than 90° (∡C > 90°) and look for a geometric way of "seeing" the defect or, the amount by which the area denoted by c^2 overshoots the area denoted by $a^2 + b^2$ -- that is $c^2 - (a^2 + b^2)$.

Mimicking the Right Triangle Case

One way of attempting the above is to try to mimic Euclid's proof for the case in which ∡C is a right angle. Since Euclid's proof is only one of well over three hundred different proofs of the Pythagorean theorem,[7] let us briefly recall some details of his proof. As suggested above, Euclid proves geometrically (i.e., makes no use of algebraic formulas for area) that the square on the side opposite the right angle is equal to the sum of the squares on the other two sides. He does

---

[7]See Elisha Loomis. *The Pythagorean Proposition,* National Council of Teachers of Mathematics, Washington, D.C., 1968.

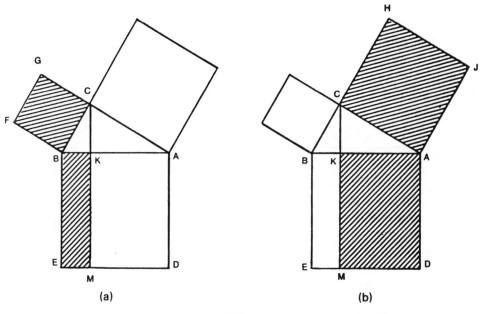

FIG. 14.

this by breaking square BADE into rectangles as shown in Figure 14(a).[8] To prove that the rectangle BKME and square BFGC are equal in area he makes use of the fact that:

ΔBEC $\cong$ ΔBAF and hence the
area of ΔBEC = area of ΔBAF. Now the
area of ΔBEC = ½BE · BK, since the length of the
altitude of ΔBEC from C is equal to BK, and the
area of ΔBAF = ½BF · CB since the length of the
altitude of ΔBAF is equal to CB.

It follows that BE·BK = BF·CB and hence that the area of rectangle BKME equals the area of square FBCG. Similarly, Euclid showed that the area of rectangle MDAK equals the area of square AJHC [Figure 14(b)].[9]

---

[8]If you have not seen the proof before, it will help you to draw in $\overline{AF}$ and $\overline{EC}$ in Figure 14a. We supply that diagram for the obtuse case in figure 16b below.

[9]We have outlined a modern version of Euclid's proof. Since Euclid did not have a marked straight edge, he was not able to denote the regions of any areas by numbers per se. Therefore, he did not have any formulas (like the product of the lengths of the base and altitude) for the areas of geometric figures; nevertheless, he was able to figure out when two figures had the "same area" by making use of the concept of congruence without invoking any concept of number. All of this is quite amazing and should give pause to anyone who claims that "Euclid must go" because of certain deficiencies. In fact, Euclid appreciated the concept of "same-area" much as Russell appreciated that of "same-number" 23 centuries later. They are both fundamental concepts for the construction of mathematical objects.

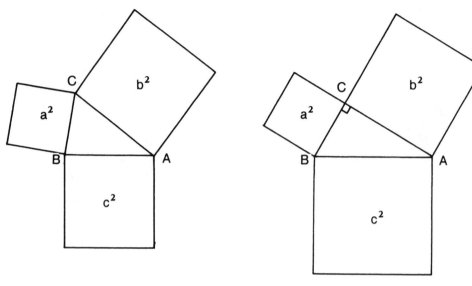

∢C < 90°

$c^2 < a^2 + b^2$

∢C = 90°

$c^2 = a^2 + b^2$

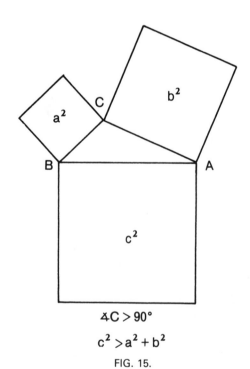

∢C > 90°

$c^2 > a^2 + b^2$

FIG. 15.

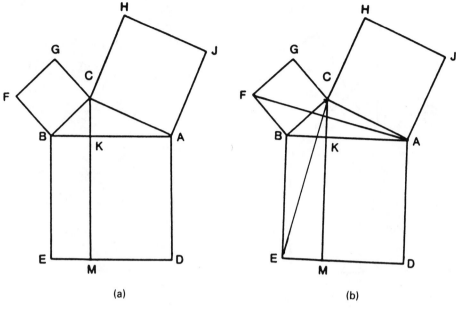

FIG. 16.

The Obtuse Angle Case

Let us now see what happens when ∡C is obtuse (Figure 16). As in the right triangle case, ∆BEC is congruent to ∆BAF and hence their areas are equal. Similarly the area of ∆BEC is ½BE·BK, since the altitude of ∆BEC is BK.

When we look at ∆BFA, and consider the base to be $\overline{BF}$, the altitude is no longer $\overline{CB}$ since ∡C is not a right angle and $\overline{ACG}$ is no longer a line segment and of course therefore neither parallel to $\overline{BF}$ nor perpendicular to $\overline{BC}$. To mimic Euclid's proof we are tempted to draw AC′G′ perpendicular to $\overline{BC}$ produced as indicated in Figure 17(a). Then the area of ∆BFA = ½·BF·C′B = ½ area BFG′C′.

Using the fact that the area of ∆BEC equals the area of ∆BAF, we conclude that the area of rectangle BEMK equals the area of rectangle BFG′C′ (rather than square BFGC). So the defect contributed by BEMK is seen to be the shaded area GCC′G′. See Figure 17(a). Similarly MDAK contributes CC″H′H. See Figure 17(b). Hence the total defect $c^2 - (a^2 + b^2)$ is seen to be the sum of the two rectangles GCC′G′ and CC″H′H. Note that this defect approaches 0 as ∡C approaches a right angle. So the Pythagorean theorem is a special case when the defect is zero. Another way of looking at it is to imagine line ACG approaching AC′G′ and line BCH approaching BC″H′ as angle C approaches a right angle.

A Step Back

Lest we lose sight of the forest for the trees, let us highlight both what we have found out so far with respect to the usefulness of problem posing and how

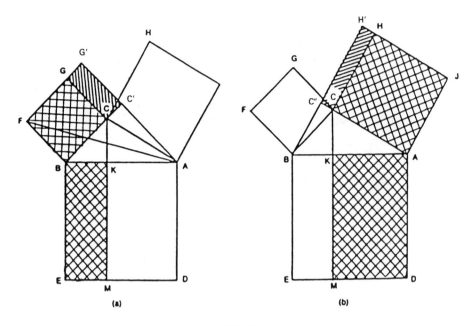

FIG. 17.

we found it out. Notice that the "What-If-Not" activity we have just been engaged in enables us to get a deeper insight into the Pythagorean theorem itself.[10] Thus, as we explore alternatives to right angles, we can appreciate that certain points are collinear in the case of a right triangle or that certain "convenient lines" form altitudes (something we took for granted before considering alternatives). Furthermore, notice that these variations on a right angle enable us to appreciate a concept in purely geometric terms which would normally require a trigonometric explanation.[11] Something special has taken place here with regard to our approach for the significance of $a^2 + b^2 < c^2$. We would like to make the nature of our analysis explicit. Notice that in attempting to locate the geometric significance of $a^2 + b^2 < c^2$, we have, as far as possible, mimicked

---

[10]Employing a proof by contradiction (on Proposition 12 and 13 of Book II and Proposition 47 of Book I of the Pythagorean theorem of Euclid), one can easily show that if $a^2 + b^2 < c^2$, then angle C is obtuse. Fig. 17 is merely a generalization of the scheme employed in Proposition 47. The total defect is shaded and is drawn on two separate figures for clarity only. See pp. 404, 405 of *Euclid's Elements* by T. L. Health, Second Edition, Dover Publications, 1956, New York.

[11]As a matter of fact, we now have the roots of an argument that explains in some sense the algebraic ideas behind the law of cosines: $c^2 = a^2 + b^2 - 2 a \cdot b \cos C$. Notice that the area of rectangle G'C'CG is $GC \cdot CC'$ which equals $-a \cdot b \cos C$ and the area of rectangle HCC"H' which equals $-b \cdot a \cos C$. Hence the total defect is $-2ab \cos C$. An additional surprise is that each of the areas on the legs contribute equally to the defect; that is, the amount by which the area on each leg fails to contribute to the exact area of its share of the square on the "hypotenuse" is the same!

the proof of the Pythagorean theorem for which $a^2 + b^2 = c^2$. The concept of analyzing the variation of a phenomenon (in this case a proof) by mimicking the original phenomenon is one that sometimes pays off in our understanding the original situation. It is a concept worth keeping in mind.

A Numerical Analysis

Next let us consider a second question in relation to, "What if $a^2 + b^2 < c^2$?" Consider $(\sim 7)_1$b. For what whole numbers is the inequality $a^2 + b^2 < c^2$ true? There are several ways to explore the problem. We might start by listing easy solutions. There are several: (1, 1, 3); (1, 1, 4); (1, 1, 5); (1, 1, 6); (1, 1, 7). Without much difficulty we can see that (1, 1, n) will satisfy the inequality for any n a natural number greater than 1. Therefore this gives an infinite number of solutions (we have, of course, still *excluded* an infinite number of possibilities).

The answer that there is an infinite number of solutions, based upon the observation that the inequality holds for all triples of the form (1, 1, n) for $n > 1$, is as unsatisfying as the observation that there is an infinite number of Pythagorean triples, based on the observation that the equality $a^2 + b^2 = c^2$ holds for all triplets of the form (3n, 4n, 5n) for any n. Just as the problem of finding the number of Pythagorean triples is made more interesting by defining *primitive* Pythagorean triples (where a, b, and c are relatively prime), so it is worthwhile to define a solution here in such a way that (1, 1, n) for all $n > 1$ represents only *one* rather than an infinite number of solutions. Given this refinement of the concept of solution, what would another solution be?

We leave $(\sim 7)_1$(c), (d) for you to explore on your own. Notice that in $(\sim 7)_1$(a) and (b), we have solved the problem of what the geometric significance of $a^2 + b^2 < c^2$ is, and we have indicated how to begin to solve the problem of what whole numbers satisfy $a^2 + b^2 < c^2$. That is, we have become involved in problem solving and problem analyzing. We call this Level IV of our scheme. We have however not yet quite finished with our technique of posing problems and so we turn to another feature in the next section.

A New Addition to the "What-If-Not" Strategy: Cycling

So far we have been systematic in listing attributes and then asking "What-If-Not?" for each. Sometimes this has made us aware of new attributes which we have then added to our list. But we have also thought of new "What-If-Nots" that were not obtainable by strictly applying methods discussed so far. In this section we indicate how a somewhat "sloppier" "What-If-Not" procedure may extend the process fruitfully. In a sense, we are going to loop through some branches of our diagram. We will need alternatives to two or more attributes to do so.

Among the many "What-If-Not" alternatives we can derive by modifying the attributes of equality (Attribute 7) and equal exponents (Attribute 9) for the Pythagorean theorem are the following respectively:

$$(\sim 7)_1: a^2 + b^2 < c^2$$

$$(\sim 9)_4: a^2 + b^2 = c.$$

Let us use these two alternatives to illustrate what else we can do to add other possibilities we cannot get by our previous methods. Notice that $(\sim 7)_1$ deals with inequality but keeps the right-hand term fixed, while $(\sim 9)_4$ keeps equality fixed but deals with an exponent of one.

A new form would be:

$$a^2 + b^2 < c.$$

It is clear that a simple, systematic application of the "What-If-Not" principle on any of the listed attributes would not yield the sentence $a^2 + b^2 < c$. There are at least two possible paths indicated in the left-hand and right-hand branches of Figure 18. We could first (see the left-hand branch) apply the "What-If-Not" principle to Attribute 7 (equality) and then reapply the same principle to Attribute 9 (three equal exponents). Or we could reverse the order and start with the right-hand branch.

The process of varying one attribute followed by varying another suggests a

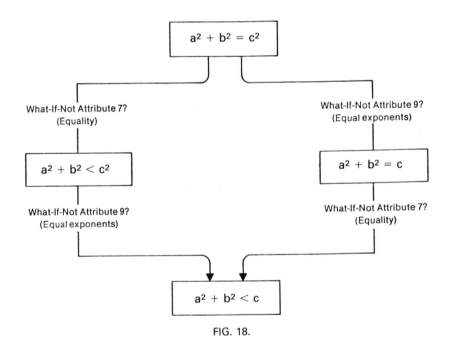

FIG. 18.

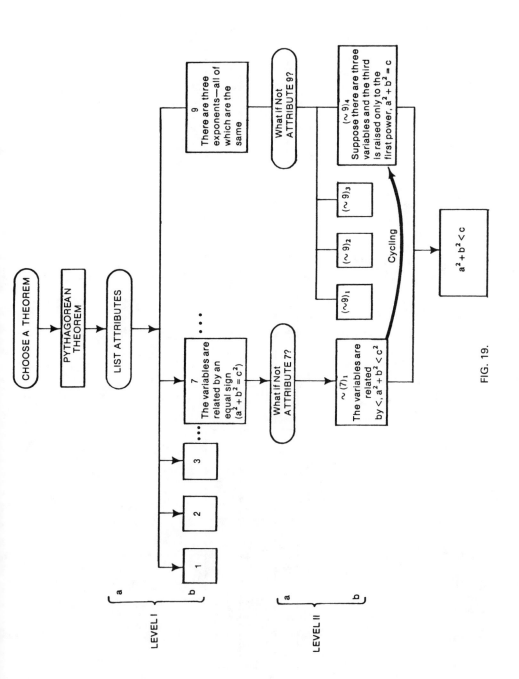

FIG. 19.

57

TABLE 3
Number of Ordered Pairs of Integers as a Function of Integral Values of c in $a^2 + b^2 < c$

c	1	2	3	4	5	6	7	8	9	10	11	12	13	14	15	16	17	18	19
(a, b): $a^2 + b^2 < c$	(0, 0)	(0, 0), (± 1, 0), (0, ± 1)	?	?	?	?	.	.	.	.	.	.	.	.	.	.	.	.	?
N = number of ordered pairs	1	5	9	9	13	21	21	21	25	29	37	37	37	45	45	45	49	57	61

58

systematic technique we could employ for brainstorming new problems. We call this technique cycling. Here we have a systematic way of generating new forms by combining the above two "What-If-Nots." Without much effort we begin to generate an enormous number of new combinations of changed attributes by cycling through various branches of the chart (Figure 13) with the "What-If-Not" principle. We can demonstrate what is involved here by placing the left-hand branch of Figure 18 in the context of the overall plan. The darkened horizontal arrow in Figure 19 indicates that we have imposed $(\sim 7)_1$ onto $(\sim 9)_4$. There is, of course, nothing special about this particular imposition, and in order to significantly increase new forms we could cycle an attribute such as $(\sim 7)_1$ throughout the chart.

Now that we have a new form, $a^2 + b^2 < c$, where can we go from here? Remember that the next step is to ask a question. What question could we ask? Instead of choosing new questions, we can select some of the questions asked in our previous variations. In $(\sim 7)_1$(a)–(d) among the questions (generalized a little) we asked the following:

How many triples are there? For what numbers will the statement be true?

Let us choose the first question above and apply it to the new form. We then have the following new problem: For any fixed value of c (c a natural number), how many ordered pairs (a, b) of integers satisfy the inequality $a^2 + b^2 < c$?

We might begin the problem most naturally by creating a table (see Table 3).

We urge you to complete the second row of the table to verify the entries in the third row.

We can make a number of observations (based upon the table).

1. The number of ordered pairs in each case in our list so far is odd.
2. From c to c + 1, the number of ordered pairs increases by either 4 or 8, or remains constant.
3. There are not more than three c's in succession that have the same number of ordered pairs for solution.

Undoubtedly, you will make a number of other observations. So far, however, we have calculated a value of N for each value of c. What happens if we explore the original (more general) question. "For any c, what is the value of N?" Here we begin to look for an explicit relationship between the entries in the first and third row. There are many ways of exploring the relation of N to c. Consider differences, sums, ratios. The latter will lead to a result that will surprise you. (The use of graph paper may help reveal why a specific ratio is approached. This may lead to some fascinating "pi-in-the-sky" thinking).

Reflections on Cycling

New forms can be obtained by cycling alternatives through the different attributes as we did to obtain $a^2 + b^2 < c$. Even with only a small number of attributes and a small number of alternatives, the number of new ideas which can be obtained is staggering. Furthermore, not only the alternative *forms,* but the *questions* themselves can be cycled, as we did in the above example. This cycling technique can be very powerful.

We will illustrate this with an example from our own experience. In the previous section, we posed the problem:

What is the graph of $a^2 + b^2 < c^2$? $[(\sim 7)_1(d)]$.

In analyzing the question, we must clarify whether we are holding some of the variables fixed or not—that is, the graph could be one, two, or three dimensional. We leave it to you to analyze this problem. Let us point out, however, that the analogous question for the case of equality (what is the graph of $a^2 + b^2 = c^2$?) was one that had *not* occurred to us at the time we originally began brainstorming on questions directly related to the Pythagorean theorem. The question, "What is the graph of . . ." can also be cycled through our other forms. In this way the problem posing strategy not only enables us to pose problems with regard to changes on what is given, but gives us a better understanding of the unmodified phenomenon as well.

Notice too, that once we observe that graphing is a phenomenon about which we have asked a new question, we can turn the question itself into an *attribute.* That is, it is only after we asked the question about graphing of $a^2 + b^2 < c^2$ that we not only realized it could be applied as a question in the case of the Pythagorean relationship, but that it can become an attribute of the Pythagorean relationship. Thus, we might add as an attribute:

$a^2 + b^2 = c^2$ is a relationship that lends itself to graphing.

You may at this point wish to add a number of questions to our "handy list of questions" from chapter 3. An obvious one suggested by the above exploration would be: What is the graph of . . .?

SUMMARY

So far we have presented an outline of a problem posing strategy that we call "What-If-Not." As we have shown, there are a number of different components (Figures 12 and 13). We illustrated the strategy by using two types of starting points—a concrete material and a theorem. Since we cannot begin without choosing a starting point, perhaps we should dignify this step by calling it Level 0 of our strategy. Our next step (Level I) was to list some attributes. We then asked, "What if each attribute were not so; what *could* it be then?" (Level II). We then used these new alternatives as a basis for asking new questions (Level III). Then we selected some of our new questions and tried to analyze or answer them. This is Level IV of our scheme. The stages of our strategy can be summarized by a few key words.

The major stages of our strategy are:

Level 0   Choosing a Starting Point
Level I   Listing Attributes
Level II   What-If-Not-ing
Level III Question Asking or Problem Posing
Level IV   Analyzing the Problem

In addition, we have shown how the strategy of cycling modified attributes and cycling questions can be incorporated into the system—resulting in a number of questions that might stagger the imagination of even the most creative thinker.

Our scheme however, is not as linear as it may seem from this list. Almost every part can (and does) affect others. A new question may trigger a new attribute, and a new attribute may in turn trigger a new question (for example). This in turn may enable you to see the original phenomenon in a new light.

It may all seem very formal the first time you read about or try the approach we have described and illustrated. You may also be overwhelmed by the number of possibilities and new problems which emerge. But when you choose your own starting point and carry out the steps outlined in this chapter, you will soon internalize the strategy implied by the different levels and you will find yourself doing a "What-If-Not" procedure naturally. After a while, you will do it in a more haphazard and less systematic way as is the case with many people who do research in mathematics. In fact, we strongly hope that you will not adopt this procedure in a mechanical way. Rather, we hope that it will provide a touchstone for a spirit of investigation and free inquiry, in a most imaginative way. We hope that this spirit will not be bound by the narrow "tunnel vision" so frequently associated with school based mathematical activity. With this in mind, we turn to a more lighthearted approach with a variety of starting points in the next chapter.

Before doing so however, you might wish to look once more at the last paragraph of the above section, "Reflections on Cycling." If you are wondering how it is that people come up with questions to ask (level III) it might pay to skim the headings of chapter 3 in the section, "Strategies for Phase-One Problem Generation."

5

The "What-If-Not" Strategy in Action

In the last chapter we used two examples to develop and describe our "What-If-Not" scheme for problem posing. Now let us employ the scheme, using several different topics or situations. Unlike our approach in the previous chapter, we shall be less exhaustive here. Instead, in order to indicate the richness of the scheme, we will focus on just a few "What-If-Not" paths based upon a listing of some of the attributes.

TWO SAMPLE "WHAT-IF-NOTS" IN SOME DETAIL

Example 1. A Sequence: Fibonacci Sequence

Brief Background

Before actually doing a "What-If-Not," we want to present some background on this fascinating topic, one which not only unites different branches of mathematics, but which relates mathematics to architecture, art and even to aesthetics. In this section we shall summarize well-known results, and will indicate sources for further investigation. In the following section, we shall assume a more playful attitude as we apply the "What-If-Not" strategy to the content of the Fibonacci sequence.

Now, look at the following sequence of numbers:

$$1, 1, 2, 3, 5, 8, 13, 21, 34, 55, 89 \ldots$$

It is generated by a very simple rule, "Starting with 1 and 1 as the first two terms, add any two adjacent terms, and the sum will yield the next one." Thus:

$$1 + 1 = 2$$
$$1 + 2 = 3$$
$$2 + 3 = 5$$
$$3 + 5 = 8.$$

Since $55 + 89 = 144$, the next term in the sequence is 144. Generate a few more terms in the infinite sequence.

This sequence was investigated originally by Fibonacci (literally, "the son of Fibo") an Italian mathematician of the 13th century. Despite its simplicity, it is one of the most intriguing mathematical sequences because it connects a number of branches of mathematics and, in addition, abounds with applications to numerous other disciplines.

All of the following phenomena are related in some way to the original sequence:

- The ratio of the length to the width of the Parthenon in Greece.
- The placement of the navel in Michelangelo's David.
- The construction of a regular pentagon using only an unmarked straightedge and a pair of compasses.
- The number of leaves in a pine cone.
- The reproduction of rabbits (appropriately conceived).
- The investigation of aesthetically appealing rectangles.

One clue that may unlock several of these diverse fields for you may be revealed by observing the *ratio* of adjacent terms (choose smaller to larger numbers to get ratios). Thus we have:

$$\frac{1}{1} \doteq 1.000$$

$$\frac{1}{2} \doteq .500$$

$$\frac{2}{3} \doteq .667$$

$$\frac{3}{5} \doteq .600$$

$$\frac{5}{8} \doteq .625$$

$$\frac{8}{13} \doteq .615$$

$$\frac{13}{21} \doteq .619$$

$$\frac{21}{34} \doteq .618$$

$$\frac{34}{55} \doteq .618$$

The sequence of ratios approaches

$$\frac{\sqrt{5} - 1}{2}$$

as a limit (which is irrational and is equal to .618 to three decimal places). That number is called the "golden ratio."[1] It turns out that the ratio of width to length of the Parthenon approximates the "golden ratio," and also that David's "belly button" is placed at approximately .618 of his total height. Why the ratio of succeeding terms of the Fibonacci sequence approaches the golden ratio and how these other "real world" phenomena relate to the golden ratio is revealed in numerous books and journals.[2] Though not essential for what follows, one way of arriving at the golden ratio is to begin with the definition of the nth term in terms of the two preceding ones. Thus $t_n = t_{n-1} + t_{n-2}$. If you divide both sides by t_{n-1} and consider ratios of terms as n gets large, you are on the right track.[3] Let us now summarize a few well-known properties of the Fibonacci sequence. Later we will examine the ramifications of modifying the sequence. In summarizing, let us begin (for the record) with (a), the "find" we have already discussed:

(a) The ratio of succeeding terms approaches

$$\frac{\sqrt{5} - 1}{2} \doteq .618$$

the "golden ratio."

(b) The *difference* between any two adjacent terms generates another Fibonacci sequence (with 0 instead of 1 as the first term).
Thus: 1, 1, 2, 3, 5, 8, 13, 21 becomes 0, 1, 1, 2, 3, 5, 8.

(c) The square of any term differs by one from the product of its two adjacent terms:

$$1, 1, 2, 3, 5, 8, 13, 21, \ldots$$

$$\begin{bmatrix} \downarrow \\ 25 \\ \hookrightarrow 24 \hookleftarrow \end{bmatrix}$$

Thus: $5^2 = 3 \cdot 8 + 1$.
Also: $13^2 = 8 \cdot 21 + 1$.

---

[1] If you take a segment of length one and break it up into segments of length x and $1 - x$ so that

$$\frac{x}{1} = \frac{1 - x}{x}$$

then each of these fractions will be the golden ratio. A rectangle with such dimensions is called a golden rectangle.

[2] For a start, see Martin Gardner, "The Multiple Fascination of the Fibonacci Sequence," *Scientific American,* March 1969, pp. 116–20; Stephen I. Brown, "From the Golden Rectangle and Fibonacci to Pedagogy and Problem Posing," *Mathematics Teacher,* March 1976, pp. 180–188. You will find a bibliography leading to other sources in these articles. In addition, there is a research journal, *The Fibonacci Quarterly,* which specializes in "fall out" of the Fibonacci sequence.

[3] The uncommon development of the quadratic equation, which ends Chapter 6, provides another clue as to how we can arrive at the ratio.

(d) The product of two adjacent terms differs by one from the product of the two terms preceding and following these terms:

$$1, 1, 2, 3, 5, 8, 13, 21, \ldots$$

$$15$$
$$16$$

Thus: $3 \cdot 5 = 2 \cdot 8 - 1$.
Also: $8 \cdot 13 = 5 \cdot 21 - 1$.

If you have not explored the Fibonacci sequence before, you may wish to investigate (a)–(d) further before moving into a "What-If-Not" mode. If so, take a few minutes out *before* we begin to list the attributes (Level I) of the Fibonacci sequence.

Beginning a "What-If-Not" on Fibonacci

What are some attributes? Recall that we generate any term after the first two by adding two adjacent terms. This definition seems so simple that we might neglect to see its essential features. As we have said earlier, it may very well be that it is only after you have done some modification at other levels of the "What-If-Not" process that you will become aware of the essential features of the phenomenon you are investigating. The following are two features (in addition to the one just mentioned) that we see as essential to the definition of the sequence:

1. We start with two given numbers.
2. The two starting numbers are both 1.

Breaking Up Attributes

Of course there are more attributes to list for the Fibonacci sequence, but first it is worth observing that we have expanded what might have been one statement into two; that is, we could have said:

3. The first two given numbers are 1 and 1.

Do you see the advantage of breaking up the attribute listing as in statements 1 and 2 rather than consolidating it as in 3? By doing so, we have signaled the possibility that at a later stage we might change not just *one* thing, but two—the *number* of "starting numbers" *and* the *value* of the starting numbers. If we had selected statement 3 as a way of listing the attribute, we might very well see only the possibility of changing the *value* of the "beginning numbers" without realizing that we might also change the *number* of beginning numbers (e.g., from two to perhaps three or four).

With this word of caution, we realize that it might have even been better to break up statement 2 into two parts as indicated here:

- The first two numbers are the same.
- The same number is 1.

After having fumbled around as described above, we realized that a good way to get started would be to list the attributes as follows:

(i)   We start with two given numbers.
(ii) These two starting numbers are the same.
(iii) The same number is 1.

More Listing

Let us now move on to other attribute listing, this time without reflecting explicitly on our wording as we did for the previous listing.

(iv) If we do *something* to any two successive numbers, we get the next number.
(v)   The something we do is an *operation*.
(vi) The operation is *addition*.

Perhaps you will find ways of breaking up attributes in a more fine-grained way than we have, so that you will be able to come up with even more interesting challenges at the next stage.

What-If-Not

Having demonstrated *some* attribute listing (Level I), let us now move to Level II: "What-If-Not." Let us select (ii) as the attribute to challenge.[4] If the first two terms were *not* the same, what might they be? Suppose we maintain natural numbers and even maintain the generating characteristic of the Fibonacci sequence, but selected 10 and 7 as the first two terms?[5]

---

[4]Note that in challenging (ii), we are also challenging (iii). It is valuable nevertheless to maintain (iii) as a separate attribute because we could conceivably focus on a Fibonacci-like sequence in which the first two starting numbers are the same, but not equal to 1. That is, we could challenge (iii) but not (ii). The reason that we have "slippage" from (ii) to (iii) here is that the attributes listed are *not* independent. It is essential that we allow for such looseness because, as we have said earlier, we may not be able to see the independence of attributes until *after* we have begun the "What-If-Not" process.

[5]At this point you might realize that we did not list the fact that the terms of the sequence were natural numbers as an attribute; you might wish to add it now.

Thus, (~ii), might be, "Suppose 10, 7 are the first two terms." We thus have the following sequence:

$$10, 7, 17, 24, 41, 65, 106, 171, \ldots$$

Now that we have modified the sequence, what might we do? Of the many questions we might ask (Level III), let us consider several that derive from our knowledge of the original sequence described in the previous subsection.

Asking Questions

(a) What limit (if any) does the ratio of succeeding terms approach?

> Moving to Level IV, we begin to analyze the problem. If we take ratios of succeeding terms, we get the following: $^{10}/_7 = 1.429$, $^7/_{17} = .412$, $^{17}/_{24} = .708$. What limit do you think is being approached? Try a few more ratios. Move far out on the sequence. The fact that $^{106}/_{171} = .620$ suggests that it is reasonable to conjecture that we are once more approaching $.618 \ldots$, the golden ratio! Is it so and if so, why? An analysis of why the *original* Fibonacci ratios approach this limit might reveal why the situation has not changed in the new sequence. It is even possible that we would understand the original limit in a new light if we were to see why it is not affected by a radical change in the first two terms. Since our object here however is to exhibit the "What-If-Not" scheme in action, rather than to provide a full-blown analysis of relevant mathematics at each point, we leave that investigation up to you. The Fibonacci references at the beginning of this chapter will provide some direction should you be interested in pursuing this issue.

We move now to yet another question to investigate on our modified sequence. Let us refer to (b) discussed earlier with regard to the *bona fide* sequence.

(b) What sequence is generated by taking the *difference* of succeeding terms?

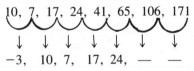

It seems clear that after a slightly rocky beginning, we once more "retrieve" the original sequence. You will probably find the analysis of *why* that is so to be easier than the analysis in (a). At any rate, the fact that we *do* arrive at a new sequence (by taking succeeding differences) that is almost identical to the original except for the first term, suggests that we *might* now investigate a totally new question that had *not* occurred to us earlier: "How can we "work backwards" given any Fibonacci-like sequence in order to discover what terms precede the first one?"

Analyzing Questions

Let us now investigate how the phenomenon described in (c) for the Fibonacci sequence fares in our new Fibonacci-like sequence. We ask the question:

(c) How does the square of any term compare with the product of its neighbors (again "borrowed" from an attribute of the original set-up)?

$$10, 7, 17, 24, 41$$
$$49$$
$$170$$

Compare 7^2 (49) with the product of its neighbors: $17 \times 10 = 170$. It is no longer the case that 7^2 differs from 10×17 by 1.

Too bad! Let us move to another question:

(d) How does the product of two adjacent terms compare with the product of the two terms preceding and following?

$$10, 7, 17, 24, 41$$

7×17 does not differ from 10×24 by 1 as in the analogous Fibonacci sequence.

Too bad once again! But wait! Look at the "miss" in both (c) and (d):

From (c): $7^2 = 10 \times 17 - 121$
From (d): $17 \times 7 = 10 \times 24 - 121$.

There is something promising here! Just as 1 was the magic number for the Fibonacci sequence, so 121 might work here. Let's try a few more cases:

$17^2 = 289$, and $24 \times 7 = 168$, again a difference $(289 - 168)$ of 121.
$24 \times 17 = 408$ and $41 \times 7 = 287$, again a difference of 121.

It looks as if we may have come upon something fascinating. Some further questions are suggested:

- Why is 121 significant here?
- How does 121 relate to our choice of 10 and 7 as our first two numbers?
- Would this magic hold for a different choice of the first two numbers?
- Of course, as in the case of examining ratios for the two sequences, we could be led back to the Fibonacci sequence itself and ask, "Why is 1 so significant as a correction factor there (just as 121 is significant for the pseudo-Fibonacci sequence)?"

- What properties (like the role of 1 and 121) are shared by the two sequences?
- Just as there was a golden rectangle associated with the Fibonacci sequence, is there a geometric figure suggested by the Fibonacci-like sequence?
- What other questions might you add?

As we suggested in chapter 4, the "What-If-Not" in this new context may raise questions that enable us to see aspects of the original context that we did not notice at first.

We could go on and on. Notice that we have made only *one variation* of an attribute (attribute ii) of the Fibonacci sequence. We modified the first two numbers. What else might we vary to pose new problems? The following are some further possible directions to investigate based on "What-If-Nots." For these questions which attributes (of the six we have listed) are we negating? Do any of these "What-If-Nots" suggest attributes that we may have neglected to list—or perhaps ones that we might break up as we did when we listed the first three? Can you figure out on which attributes we have performed a "What-If-Not" on in coming up with the following?

- What would the consequences be of adding three successive numbers to get the next term?
- What would the consequences be of adding every other number?
- Suppose we modify the operation from addition to something else? Then . . . (the question to be posed is left for you).

This is just the beginning. You can continue to make additional variations and to pose new questions based on these variations.

Example 2. A Problem: Rectangles

You may think that the previous example gave rise to rich ideas only because it was special or particularly interesting. Let us see next how our ideas can reap rewards even when we start with a very basic problem—one that may even look extremely dull, an example of a very standard type of exercise:

Calculate the area of a rectangle given that the width is 2 meters and the length is 3 meters.

Even a touch of the "What-If-Not" technique can enrich this simple exercise. Let us being by considering the problem just stated and listing a few of its attributes (Level I activity). What does your list of attributes look like? Our list, which may look quite different from yours, follows:

1. The situation is an exercise.
2. The exercise is a request to calculate.
3. The exercise deals with a four-sided shape.
4. The exercise deals with a rectangle.
5. We are asked to calculate an area.
6. The width and length are specified.
7. We are given two numbers.
8. We are asked to calculate one number.

Notice, once more, the list does not consist of attributes that are independent of each other. Nor do we rule out obvious or perhaps meaningless attributes because some of them may lead to worthwhile explorations or because they may suggest additional attributes. For example, you might think that Attribute 8 is silly, but it focuses our attention on the fact that we are probably going to give the answer as 6 square meters and not as 2×3 square meters—though it surely is worthwhile to examine the answer in factored form for some purposes.

Let us now proceed to Level II and ask "What-If-Not?" for the attributes.[6] Here we will choose only *one* attribute to illustrate our strategy. Attribute 6 on our list:

6. The width and length are specified.

"What-If-Not" Attribute 6? denoted by ($\sim$6)? What alternatives occur to you?

Here are some we have thought of:

($\sim$6)$_1$ Only the width is specified.

($\sim$6)$_2$ Only the length is specified.

($\sim$6)$_3$ The sum of the width and length is specified.

($\sim$6)$_4$ The length and width can be chosen from two given numbers.

($\sim$6)$_5$ The lengths of the two diagonals are given.

($\sim$6)$_6$ The distances from the center to the four corners are given.

---

[6]You may wish to refer back to Figure 11 of chapter 4.

$(\sim 6)_7$ The distances from the center to three corners are given.

$(\sim 6)_8$ The distances from the center to two corners are given.

$(\sim 6)_9$ The distances from any point in the rectangle to three corners are given.

$(\sim 6)_{10}$ The area is given.

Here, again, we have neither made the alternatives independent of each other nor have we ruled them out just because they seem to give insufficient or redundant information.

Let us look at one of the alternatives suggested by $(\sim 6)_4$.

$(\sim 6)_4$: The length and width can be chosen from two given numbers.

What questions might we ask now? (Such questions asking is our Level III activity.) The original question asked us to find *the* area. Here we are first faced with the question, "What are the possible rectangles?" and a new one, "How many possible rectangles are there?" This makes us more fully aware that we had only one possible rectangle before—a 2 meter by 3 meter one, since the width was specified as 2 m and the length as 3 m. Even if we now agree to consider a 3 × 2 rectangle to be the same as 2 × 3 one, we still have a more complicated problem than the original one. See Figure 20.

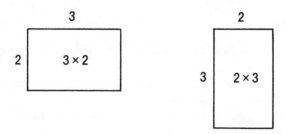

FIG. 20.

By stating that the length and width are to be *chosen* from the two lengths 2 m, 3 m, rather than being told that the length is 3 and the width 2 m, how is the situation made more interesting? What possible rectangles can we have now? Notice that we can have a 2 × 2 or a 3 × 3 square as well as a 2 × 3 rectangle. That is, we can have three possible different rectangles and two of them are squares. We can find the area of each of these rectangles.

Let us continue to ask questions on the same "What-If-Not" Attribute 6, alternative $(\sim 6)_4$. It is tempting to stick to the same question (how many rect-

TABLE 4
Number of Different Rectangles As A Function of the Number
of Starting Lengths

Number of Different Starting Sides	Number of Squares	Number of Non-square Rectangles	Total Number of Rectangles
1	1	0	1
2	2	1	3
3	3	3	6
4	4	?	?
5	5	?	?

angles?) for a moment and answer it for three different available lengths, and even for four or only one.

Suppose we had three different lengths to choose from, say lengths of a, b, c.[7] How many different rectangles can be made now? There are several ways to get the answer. How would you do it?

One way is to first determine the number of squares as we did before. In this case there are three squares: a × a, b × b, c × c. Then there are three different non-square rectangles, a × b, a × c, b × c, giving six different rectangles in all. How many different rectangles are possible if we have only one or only two different starting lengths? Let us begin to make a table to collect the information (Table 4).

What is your guess about the number of different rectangles if we had four or five different starting lengths?

If we had four possible starting lengths, we have four possible squares. How many non-square rectangles are there? We can have a choice of four different lengths for one side, and then a choice of three different lengths for the second side, giving us twelve (4 × 3) choices in all. But wait a minute; we must divide this answer by two because we decided to consider an a × b rectangle to be the same as a b × a rectangle. So, we have four squares and six non-square rectangles, yielding ten different rectangles in all. Fill in the rest of the table; do you see some patterns emerging?

Filling in a few more rows will probably persuade you that the number of different rectangles possible for n different starting lengths is $\dfrac{n(n+1)}{2}$ or some

---

[7]Using variables here made us realize that another attribute is, "We are given specific numbers." In this case, we decided to use variables rather than specific numbers for brevity of presentation rather than as a consequence of consciously applying the "What-If-Not" strategy.

equivalent formula.[8] One way to show that this is the correct result is to realize that there are n possible squares and $\dfrac{n(n-1)}{2}$ different rectangles that are not squares. This gives a total of n $+ \dfrac{n(n-1)}{2} = \dfrac{n(n+1)}{2}$ different rectangles.[9]

Returning to our original question about areas, we can now calculate the area of each possible rectangle for any given value of n (the number of different starting lengths). Before looking at the general cases, you might want to find all possible areas for four starting lengths of 3, 5, 7, and 10 respectively. Then see Table 5.

We can now ask a new question, "For any given value of n (e.g., n = 4) which rectangle has the smallest area? Which has the greatest area?" It is easy to answer these questions if we assume a < b < c < d, since a^2 is clearly the smallest and d^2 the largest value for the area. It is also easy to see that $a^2 <$ ab < $b^2 <$ bc < $c^2 <$ cd < d^2, but it is not trivial to analyze where ac, ad and bd belong in this sequence. What conditions do you have to impose on the relative sizes of a, b, c or d to make a definitive statement? Of course, for any four particular lengths, you can calculate the areas and arrange the rectangles according to size. Try a few different values of a, b, c, d to see if you can get the orders of the rectangles changed. Under what conditions on a, b, c, d is the size of the

---

[8]The numbers 1, 3, 6, 10, 15, 21, . . . are called triangular numbers. Note that 1 = 1, 3 = 1 + 2, 6 = 1 + 2 + 3, 10 = 1 + 2 + 3 + 4. If we denote the triangular numbers by T_1, T_2, T_3, . . ., T_n , then T_n = 1 + 2 + 3 + . . . + n = n(n + 1)/2. Each T_n can be represented by dots that form a triangular pattern; for example

T_3 . . . T_4 . . . . T_5 . . . . .
. .   . .
.   . .   . . .
.   .

If you have never proved the formula for T_n, you can convince yourself of its correctness by taking a staircase of squares depicting 1 + 2 + 3 + 4 + 5 for example. Then make a duplicate of it. Can you put them together to form a rectangle? How many square are there in the rectangle?

[9]Look at table 4. Can you see why the number of non-square rectangles for say, four different lengths is 3 + 3, i.e., 1 + 2 + 3, and for 5 different lengths is 6 + 4, i.e., 1 + 2 + 3 + 4?

TABLE 5
Areas as a Function of Starting Lengths

Number of Starting Sides, n	Number of Squares	Number of Non-square Rectangles	Total Number of Rectangles	Areas
1: (a)	1	0	1	a^2
2: (a,b)	2	1	3	a^2, b^2 ab
3: (a,b,c)	3	3	6	a^2, b^2, c^2 ab, ac, bc
4: (a,b,c,d)	4	6	10	a^2, b^2, c^2 ab, ac, ad bc, bd cd
$n: (s_1, s_2, \ldots s_n)$	n	$\dfrac{n(n-1)}{2}$	$\dfrac{n(n+1)}{2}$	

areas of the two rectangles a × c and b × d reversed? the same? Next, you may wish to tackle the ordering according to area of the fifteen possible rectangles made from five starting lengths.

Notice that the problem, "How many different rectangles are possible to make from a given number of different lengths?" is a practical one. Carpenters, for example, may meet such a problem when they need to know how many different sized frames they can produce from different available lengths. They may need to know how many different lengths they must stock to be able to make, say, fifteen different sized frames for items such as waterbeds, door frames, window molding and picture frames. They might be quite surprised to find that to make sixteen different frames, they need to stock six different lengths but that this enables them to make twenty-one different sized frames! Notice, we have not yet taken into consideration that some frames may be different in size and yet have the same area.

We have pursued only one small path for one changed attribute and only a tiny fraction of the alternatives to that situation.[10] We asked only a very few questions. Do you realize how many new paths the original question suggests? Where are you led if you pursue a "What-If-Not" on Attribute 4?

Attribute 4. The exercise deals with a rectangle.

What if it did not deal with a rectangle? Suppose it dealt with a triangle, a rhombus or a general quadrilateral? Where would old and new questions lead? It

---

[10]For further details see Marion Walter, "Frame Geometry: An Example in Posing and Solving Problems," *The Arithmetic Teacher*, October 1980, pp. 16–18; and Marie Kuper and Marion Walter, "From Edges to Solids," *Mathematics Teaching*, No. 74, March 1976, pp. 20–23.

should be clear that starting with a mundane example of calculating the area of one particular rectangle, we can, by just a touch of the "What-If-Not" technique open up the problem to investigations of various depths and degrees of difficulty.

OTHER BEGINNINGS: SOME SNIPPETS

This section is intended to entice you with the spirit of the "What-If-Not" strategy making use of the various levels, recalled here:

Level I   Attribute Listing
Level II   "What-If-Not-ing"
Level III Question Asking
Level IV Analyzing a Problem

Without specifying in much detail which specific level is being used, we present these snippets to indicate the unexpected byways we have been led to explore as a result of "What-If-Not-ing" on a variety of starting points. A major reason for presenting these snippets is to encourage you to use your own starting points.

Our experience indicates that there are significant differences among people in their ability to use the strategy implicitly. For some people, considerable practice is needed before learning to challenge the given in any situation; for others, relatively little explicit teaching is necessary. You may wish to take this observation into consideration as you approach some of the situations described here.

It has also been our experience that most people eventually do not require the overt "What-If-Not" structure to generate new problems because the method is incorporated into their thinking. Though you will uncover interesting issues and topics that never occurred to us in our explorations of the situations that follow, we have indicated in each case something for you to read in the event that you wish to compare your explorations with someone else's. In some cases the explorations will be very open-ended; in others, we will direct you in ways that are rather specific and closed.

Some Data[11]

How often have you caught yourself daydreaming over a doodle of some kind or even over some arithmetic calculation? The following is some very unexpected fall-out based on a "What-If-Not" perspective imposed on just such a situation.

---

[11]See Stephen I. Brown, "A New Multiplication Algorithm: On the Complexity of Simplicity," *Arithmetic Teacher*, Nov. 1975, pp. 546–54 and "A Musing on Multiplication," *Mathematics Teaching*, 1974, 61, pp. 26–30.

Look at the following number pattern that was arrived at in a spirit of doodling:

$$1 \times 3 = 3$$
$$2 \times 4 = 8$$
$$3 \times 5 = 15$$
$$4 \times 6 = 24$$
$$5 \times 7 = 35$$

There are many attributes to observe in the above. For example, notice that:

1. In each case there are two factors.
2. The factors in each pair differ by 2.
3. The differences between the products form an interesting pattern:

$$8 - 3 = 5$$
$$15 - 8 = 7$$
$$24 - 15 = 9$$
$$35 - 24 = 11$$

It appears that the differences form an arithmetic progression; in addition, the products alternate in parity (odd, even, odd, even, odd). You could take these data and generate many observations, conjectures or questions in the spirit of chapter 3, in which we accept the given.

We could also do a "What-If-Not" on the data in the spirit of chapter 4. With the intention of carrying out such an exploration, let us list one more attribute that was the impetus for this investigation. First look once more at 3, 8, 15, 24, and 35 . . . as the start of a sequence. If you think in metaphors like "striving," you will be impressed that those numbers in the sequence are all *almost* perfect squares. They all miss by one. Here is the picture:

$$1 \times 3 = 3 \rightarrow 4 \text{ (missing by one)}$$
$$2 \times 4 = 8 \rightarrow 9 \text{ (missing by one)}$$
$$3 \times 5 = 15 \rightarrow 16 \text{ (missing by one)}$$
$$4 \times 6 = 24 \rightarrow 25 \text{ (missing by one)}$$
$$5 \times 7 = 35 \rightarrow 36 \text{ (missing by one)}$$

To see where this might lead, let us focus on the attribute that asserts that the factors differ by two. Suppose they are made to differ by four. Then if we still start with 1, we have:

$$1 \times 5 = 5$$
$$2 \times 6 = 12$$
$$3 \times 7 = 21$$
$$4 \times 8 = 32$$
$$5 \times 9 = 45$$

So what? In using the "What-If-Not" strategy we have to ask a question, something we have not done yet. Let us choose as a question something that comes out of the last attribute we observed earlier, that the pattern almost yields squares. Let us ask, "Can we get that again?"

$$1 \times 5 = 5 = \textcircled{4} + 1$$
$$2 \times 6 = 12 = \textcircled{9} + 3$$
$$3 \times 7 = 21 = \textcircled{16} + 5$$
$$4 \times 8 = 32 = \textcircled{25} + 7$$
$$5 \times 9 = 45 = \textcircled{36} + 9$$

Though this pattern yields squares, the correction factors form an arithmetic progression $(1, 3, 5, 7, 9)$. In our original metaphor of "striving," the correction factor for all numbers was the same, namely the number 1. Can we find something like that here? If we try for nine rather than four as the "striven square" for 1×5, let's see what emerges.

$$1 \times 5 = 5 = \textcircled{9} - 4 = 3^2 - 2^2$$
$$2 \times 6 = 12 = \textcircled{16} - 4 = 4^2 - 2^2$$
$$3 \times 7 = 21 = \textcircled{25} - 4 = 5^2 - 2^2$$
$$4 \times 8 = \quad ?$$
$$5 \times 9 = \quad ?$$

Notice that here we have the same correction factor in every case—four. Furthermore, that correction factor itself is a perfect square! As we look back at the original data, we realize that there too the correction factor (1) is also a perfect square.

At this point, you are probably tempted to explore another variation of the product pairs. Again, let us strive for squares given the following factors. (What kind of number is the correction factor itself?)

$$1 \times 7 = 7 = \textcircled{4^2} - ???$$
$$2 \times 8 = 16 = \textcircled{5^2} - ???$$

Finish up on your own!

There is a lot to explore just following this particular line of thought. Can you calculate 5×13 so that the "striven number" and the correction factor are both squares? Can you find those squares in an efficient manner?

If you think of the two numbers as sitting on the ends of a see-saw, then it is easy to figure out how to create the two squares. The following picture suggests what is happening. Nine is midway between 5 and 13, thus "balancing" 5 and 13. It is easy to see that the correction factor is 4.

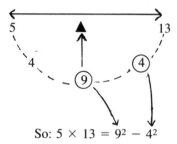

So: $5 \times 13 = 9^2 - 4^2$

The implications of this search are extraordinary; they suggest, ultimately, a new algorithm for multiplying *any* two natural numbers. The search was in fact begun by doing a "What-If-Not" based on free-floating musing as a start. You might want to investigate whether this newly emerging procedure (multiplying any two numbers in terms of the difference of squares) actually becomes complicated or not. It is much more manageable than you would guess initially.

Before leaving this activity, you might also want to do at least one more "What-If-Not" on the data to see if you can find another starting path, based on your own muse. It might be worth saving your future doodles to see in what unexpected directions later "What-If-Nots" might take you.

Starting With a Problem

Given a point P in the interior of rectangle ABCD, such that PA = 3, PB = 4, PC = 5 (Figure 21). What is PD?[12] We decided to use this textbook problem as a starting point for "What-If-Not-ing" because we were surprised by the nature of the problem.

Actually, it was more discomfort than surprise that piqued our interest at the beginning, because the sides of the rectangle were not given. How is it possible to determine the length of the fourth segment $\overline{PD}$ without knowing the lengths of the sides? Further analysis revealed the surprising result that despite the fact that the length of $\overline{PD}$ is indeed determined (PD = $3\sqrt{2}$), there are an infinite number of rectangles satisfying the given conditions. That piqued our interest enough to

[12]This problem as stated appears in Alan R. Hoffer, *Geometry*, Menlo Park, Addison-Wesley, 1979, Problem 45, p. 526. It is developed in a What-If-Not spirit in Marion Walter, "Exploring a Rectangle Problem," *Mathematics Magazine*, 54, 3 May 1981, pp. 131–134.

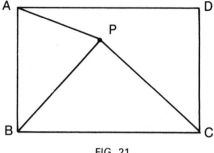

FIG. 21.

suggest using the problem as a starting point for a "What-If-Not." So we looked again at Figure 21 and made a list of attributes including:

1. The problem deals with a rectangle.
2. The problem deals with a four-sided shape.
3. The problem deals with a shape that has four equal angles.
4. The number of lengths given is one less than the number of vertices.
5. The lengths of the three segments from one point to three vertices are given.

We realized that by focusing on each part of sentence number 5 in turn—The *lengths* of the *three segments* from *one point* to *three vertices* are given—we actually had many attributes within that one! We capture that find by expanding our list to include attributes 6–12.

6. The *lengths* of the three segments, are given.
7. The lengths of *three* segments are given.
8. The lengths of three *segments* are given.
9. The lengths of segments starting from *one* point are given.
10. The lengths of segments starting from one *point* are given.
11. The lengths of segments terminating at *three* vertices are given.
12. The lengths of segments terminating at *vertices* are given.

Instead of listing some "What-If-Nots" on these few attributes, we have instead drawn pictures (Figure 22) to suggest some alternatives. For example, Figure 22(a) negates the fact that a four-sided figure is given, while Figure 22(b) negates the fact that the number of lengths given is one less than the number of vertices. Which attributes are negated by other figures?

Now look at the diagrams in Figure 22 and use them as a catalyst to pose a

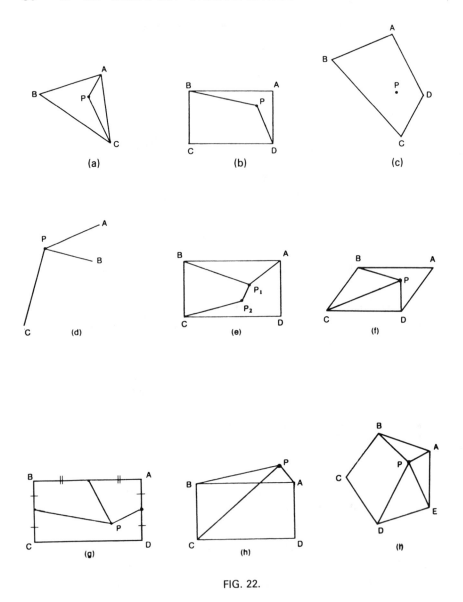

FIG. 22.

question or two. You may wish to recycle old questions—ones posed about the original diagram—or the new diagrams may suggest different questions.

What questions can you pose for each picture? Can you recycle some old questions? Which new ones occur to you?

Long Division: An Algorithm[13]

We have all slaved over some form of long division (at least in our youth!). There are many things to observe about the long-division algorithm. One attribute is that the remainder is always less than the divisor. Thus:

$$17\overline{)4266} = \text{number} + \text{a remainder}$$

and the remainder is smaller than 17. Below is the calculation of Sharon, a fourth-grade student first learning the algorithm. She got stuck when she did not know how to divide 17 into 16.

$$
\begin{array}{r}
25 \\
17\overline{)4266} \\
34 \\
\hline
86 \\
85 \\
\hline
16
\end{array}
$$

Then her eyes lit up and she commented, "If I had to divide 17 into 17, instead of into 16, I could do it. I would get 1 as a part of the answer. I'm going to make believe that I do have 17 instead of 16 for a minute." She then put 1 in the quotient and wrote -1 next to it to indicate that she had to subtract 1 from the product of 251 and 17 to get the check of 4266 as a correct answer. The work she did was:

$$
\begin{array}{r}
251 \; (-1) \\
17\overline{)4266} \\
34 \\
\hline
86 \\
85 \\
\hline
16 \\
17
\end{array}
$$

What do you think of her procedure? How would you check to determine whether or not the answer is correct? Will the implied new algorithm work in other cases? What attributes of the long division algorithm are challenged by her procedure? What questions does it raise for you?

Explore a few more division problems with negative remainders yourself!

It is worth observing that Sharon has come up with something that may not be merely a cute trick, but which has a more radical potential. In a sense, she has

---

[13]Stephen I. Brown, "Sharon's 'Kye'," *Mathematics Teaching*, No. 94, March 1981, pp. 11–17.

devised an original way of doing long division. What she has done is analogous to what a third grader did several years ago for the case of the standard subtraction algorithm. Here is an account of that similar experience:

> A few years ago, in the elementary school in Weston, Connecticut, a third-grade boy named Kye invented a new algorithm for subtracting. His teacher had been solving the problem:

$$\begin{array}{r} 64 \\ -28 \\ \hline \end{array}$$

> and had said, "We can't subtract eight from four, so we have to regroup the sixty as . . ." At this point Kye interrupted, took the chalk, and did this:

	Kye wrote:
Kye said:	64
"Oh, yes, you can! Four minus eight is	-28
negative four . . .	-4

	64
	-28
	-4
. . .and sixty minus twenty is forty . . .	40

	64
	-28
	-4
	40
. . . and forty and negative four are thirty-six,	36

so the answer is thirty-six."[14]

You may be asking yourself how these examples relate to the "What-If-Not" scheme. It is obvious from the description that neither Sharon nor Kye was attempting *explicitly* to do a "What-If-Not" on the standard algorithms. Their approaches were born more out of a sense of desperation (for Sharon) and innocence (for Kye). Though neither of them made explicit use of the "What-If-Not" strategy, their creative responses can inspire *us* to perform a "What-If-Not." The major contribution each of them has made is to challenge implicitly the assumption (in several places) that we must make use of only *positive* integers in calculating differences and quotients. It is thus possible for each of us to become aware and to take advantage of other people's challenges to the

---

[14]Robert Davis, "The Misuse of Educational Objectives," *Educational Technology*, Nov. 1973, pp. 34–36.

existing order of things, even when they themselves may be unaware of the radical potential of what they have done.

A beginning list of attributes for their alternative approaches then might involve something like:

1. The intermediate stages of the calculation all involve positive integers.
2. The answer in all cases is a positive integer (or combination of positive integers).

Notice that an advantage of listing the attributes like this is that now we are led to explore not only the use of negative numbers as Sharon and Kye have done, but other possibilities (such as fractions) as well. A valuable fall-out of this discussion is that it exhibits a point we have suggested earlier with regard to the "What-If-Not" scheme—namely, that the levels feed on each other in unanticipated ways. In this case, we see how the inadvertent varying of an attribute can make us explicitly aware of the attribute in the first place, thus standing on its head what would appear to be a more expected, logical order of things.

As we suggested earlier, the value of such "What-If-Not" analysis is not merely the potential it raises for creative activity; there is also value in the insight we can develop with regard to the accepted algorithms. Both students made us aware that we have assumed that the domain for calculation, as well as for answers, is that of the natural numbers, and not that of the negative integers. Even those who have studied number theory and know the long-division algorithm as a more general theorem about quotients and remainders, may know the logical derivations but not appreciate the *significance* that remainders are located uniquely in the range between 0 and the divisor (so that we expect a remainder to be between 0 and 16 in Sharon's example). To understand the significance of such observations, we must find out not only how to prove theorems but we must also realize the consequences of violating the essential conditions of the theorem. Both of these youngsters invite us to do exactly that. We leave the exploration of the significance of Kye's and Sharon's finds for your enjoyment.

A Construction: The Usual Regular Hexagon Construction Using a Straightedge and Compass[15]

Once we know how to do something in one way, we may tend to stop thinking about it further. Generally, we do not even ask ourselves why it works. Of course, for many routine activities we do not want to have to think about them; we want to be able to do them automatically so that we can use them for purposes

---

[15]Marion Walter, "Do We Rob Students of a Chance to Learn?" *For the Learning of Mathematics,* Vol. 1, No. 3, March 1981, pp. 16–18.

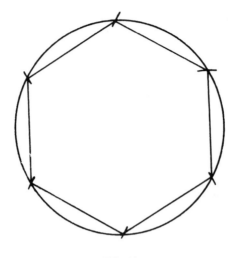

FIG. 23.

of exploring new problems or to satisfy someone who wants to test our ability to recall associated skills. Certainly this is the case for the standard hexagon construction shown in Figure 23, especially if our goal is to reproduce a solution quickly and/or on demand. Still, it is worthwhile to stop to examine even such a routine construction using the "What-If-Not" technique, when we have a quiet moment and wish to explore, rather than merely respond to someone else's demands. What are some attributes of the hexagon construction in Figure 23? They include:

1. The polygon formed is a regular hexagon.
2. Only straightedge and compass were used.
3. The end result is a drawing.
4. A circle was used.
5. *One* circle was used.
6. Six arcs were drawn on the circle.
7. It assumed that the student knew how to do it.
8. It requires accuracy.
9. It basically makes use of 60° angles.

Figure 24 shows some drawings which suggest alternate ways of constructing regular hexagons and new related objects on which to pose questions about construction. For example, Figure 24(a) might suggest the question, "How can you construct a regular hexagon without drawing a circle?" Figure 24(d) might prompt you to ask, "How can you use a circle to find a different construction?"

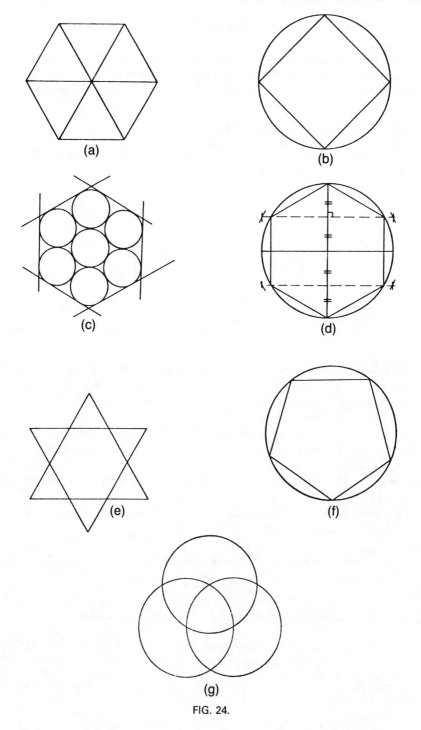

FIG. 24.

Figure 24(e) may suggest asking how overlapping equilateral triangles can make a hexagon.

Now that you have examined these drawings in the spirit of a "What-If-Not," you have probably uncovered several properties of a regular hexagon that you had not been aware of when you made use of only the standard construction.

Another Problem: An Inscribed Square

Find the area of the square that is inscribed in a right triangle such that it has one side on the base of the triangle (Figure 25a).

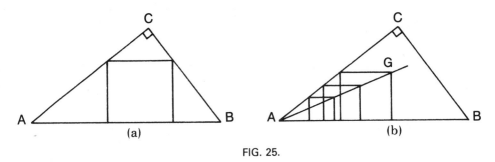

(a)   (b)

FIG. 25.

In solving this problem you have to decide what really is being asked for in the request to inscribe a square. George Polya has an elegant discussion of the problem of inscribing a square in a right triangle.[16] He points out that the squares with one side on the base of the triangle and with one vertex on the side AC of the triangle ABC are related by an enlargement (dilation) with center A. Hence the "free" fourth vertex (e.g., G) of each square of the family of squares will lie on a straight line through A and G (Figure 25b). To construct the fourth vertex of the required inscribed square, all you have to do is to construct the intersection of AG and CB.

The situation is ripe with possibilities for a "What-If-Not" approach, so we can begin by listing some attributes[17]:

1. The problem deals, in part, with a triangle.
2. The problem deals with a *right* triangle.
3. The problem deals with an *inscribed* figure.
4. The inscribed figure is a square.

[16]George Polya, *How To Solve It*. Princeton: Princeton University Press, 1973, pp. 23–25; it is also mentioned in George Polya, *Mathematical Discovery: On Understanding, Learning and Teaching Problem Solving*, Vol. I. New York: John Wiley and Sons, 1962, p. 18 and p. 155.

[17]Marion Walter, "A Few Steps Down the Path of a Locus Problem," *Mathematics Teaching*, 53, 1970, pp. 23–25.

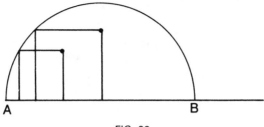

FIG. 26.

5. The inscribed figure is to have one side on the base of the triangle.
6. The problem deals with the *area* of the square.
7. The outside shape is a triangle.
8. Two *different* shapes are involved.
9. The shapes are in the plane.

After looking at this list you might wonder "What-If-Not" number 6? What could the problem deal with if not with area? A common alternative people choose is perimeter. However, because of Polya's use of loci to solve the original problem, we were led to think about loci in doing a "What-If-Not." Thus, we make the substitution "the problem deals with loci" in Attribute 6. We choose to look at the locus on the fourth vertex of the square. It is a straight line as we saw earlier. You may not find that fact interesting, but it led us to ask questions about loci under alternate possibilities.

For example, look at attribute 1. (See Figure 26.) What if the triangle were not a triangle? Suppose first that it is a semicircle. (The "base" of the triangle becomes a diameter and the "roof" is changed.) What is the locus of the fourth (free) vertex?

Or suppose we maintain the original figure as a semicircle, and create an inscribed figure which is not a square, but a circle. See Figure 27. What is the locus of the centers?

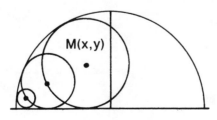

FIG. 27.

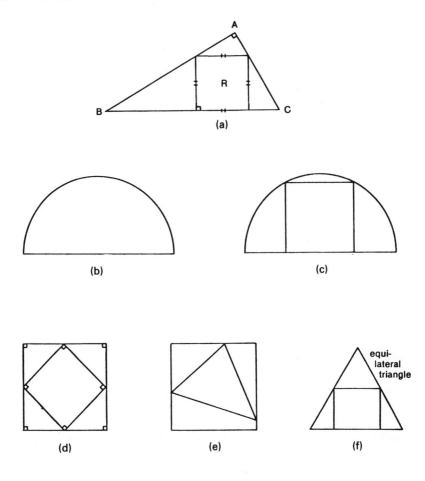

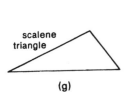

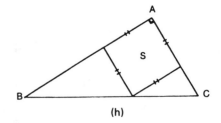

FIG. 28.

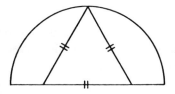
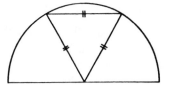

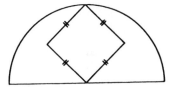

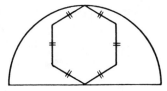
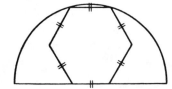

FIG. 29.

We next considered several alternatives—several "What-If-Nots" on our partial list of attributes—and we drew pictures. You may wish to add to the array of pictures after forming your own attributes and your own "What-If-Nots."

The first drawing in Figure 28 indicates the problem as given. Figure 28(b) through 28(h) show some of our alternatives. For each picture in Figure 28, we could ask a question about the areas, perimeters, or loci, or even about some other concept, for there are numerous questions to ask. What questions occur to you?

Polya investigates both cases (a) and (h) of Figure 28. We decided to compare the two areas of the squares—R and S. We were surprised when we found that $1/R - 1/S = 1$ if we take the hypotenuse of the right triangle to be of unit length. Just seeing these two squares inscribed in this way made us think of other diagrams. Do the diagrams in Figure 29 encourage you to pose some further problems?

An Activity: Looking at Boxes

We are surrounded by boxes of many different shapes and sizes, made in different ways and fabricated out of numerous types of materials. Have you ever wondered how they are made? Actually, there are a surprising number of practical and theoretical problems to consider when pondering this question. Suppose we idealize the situation and start by considering a cubical box made of six squares and no flaps. How do you think this box could be put together from one connected piece of cardboard? Try to visualize it![18]

The first one most people draw looks like this:

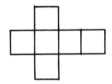

Some people draw a different one, or more than one pattern. Check to see if the two patterns in Figure 30 fold into a cube. Just finding all the possible patterns that fold into a cube (still ignoring flaps) is a problem in itself. Since the problem of six squares is quite an involved one, let us step back and consider instead the somewhat simpler one of investigating all possible patterns for making a box without a top, a five-sided box in the shape of a cube. Figure 31(a) shows a few of them. There are eight possible patterns that fold into a cubical box without a top, if you agree to count two shapes, such as shown in Figure 31(b) as the "same" because they are congruent. (You can get one from the other by "flipping.")

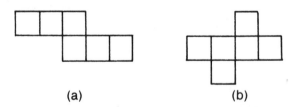

(a)   (b)

FIG. 30.

Now that we have slightly simplified the task, let us complicate life by returning to the original one. We will list some attributes of the original activity—that of arranging six squares that fold into a cubical box.

---

[18]Marion Walter, "Polyominoes, Milk Cartons and Groups," *Mathematics Teaching*, 53. Summer 1968, p. 12–19; "A Second Example of Informal Geometry: Milk Cartons," *Arithmetic Teacher*, Vol. XVI, No. 5, May 1969, pp. 368–370. Some of the ideas from both of these articles appear in *Boxes, Squares and Other Things: A Teacher's Guide to a Unit on Informal Geometry*, Reston, VA National Council of Teachers of Mathematics, 1970.

1. There are six squares.
2. Whole edges are touching.
3. The squares are congruent.
4. The pattern folds into a solid.
5. The pattern has congruent faces.
6. The solid is regular.
7. The solid is a cube.
8. The shapes are quadrilaterals.
9. The shapes are rectangles (and are squares).
10. The segments are straight.
11. The pattern is in the plane.
12. All the shapes are of one kind.
13. Two patterns are given.
14. The faces are regular.

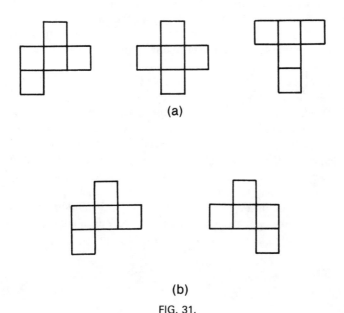

(a)

(b)

FIG. 31.

Now here are a few questions that can come from a ''What-If-Not'' on this list of attributes and from asking either new questions or recycling old ones.

1. What other solids can you make that have six congruent faces?
2. What six-sided shapes can you make that have six faces, none of which are quadrilaterals?
3. What six-faced shapes can you make from parallelograms?
4. What solids can you make from squares that do not have six faces?
5. How would you recycle all of the above replacing six by five?
6. What solids can you create with equilateral triangles?

Having started with the rather limited problem of how many square patterns there are that fold into a cubical box, we have widened our explorations considerably.

Prime Numbers[19]

The concept of prime number is a central one in number theory. Recall that a number is prime if it has exactly two different divisors. So 2, 3, 5, 7, 11 are the first few primes in the set of natural numbers. Prime numbers have a history that goes back a long way. Over 2,000 years ago, Euclid settled the question of how many there are by proving that there must be an infinite number of primes—a proof that is brief but one of the most elegant mathematical proofs.

Knowing that there are an infinite number of prime numbers immediately suggests that we might be interested in finding some simple formula that would always yield a prime.

Mathematical thought was devoted to a search for such a formula for a long period of time. In the 16th through the 18th century, men of the caliber of Mersenne, Fermat, and Euler each had some interesting simple formulas that supposedly generated primes (e.g., $2^{(2^n)} + 1$, $n^2 + n + 41$) but that also broke down at certain points. In 1947, Mills produced a formula that he proved would always yield primes. He showed that $[a^{3^n}]$ had to work for a fixed a and for every natural number n.[20] The "joke," as you would expect, is that no one knows what a must be; it is only known that there must *exist* such an a.

One interesting and unsolved problem was created by Goldbach in the early 18th century. He came up with a conjecture that every even number greater than two can be represented as the sum of two primes. Thus:

$$4 = 2 + 2$$

$$6 = 3 + 3$$

[19]See Stephen I. Brown, "Of 'Prime' Concern: What Domain," *Mathematics Teacher,* May 1965, pp. 402–7; "'Prime' Pedagogical Schemes," *American Mathematical Monthly,* 75, 6, June–July 1968, pp. 660–664. Some of the ideas from these articles also appear in *Some Prime Comparisons.* Reston, VA, National Council of Teachers of Mathematics, 1978.

[20]The definition of [x] is that it is the greatest integer less than or equal to x. So [3.7] = 3.

$$12 = 7 + 5$$
$$18 = 7 + 11$$

In a period of over 250 years, no one has either proven or disproved that conjecture, though interesting (and sometimes humorous) headway has been made on the problem.

There are many properties about prime numbers that do not generate either the mysteriousness of Goldbach's conjecture or the tantalizing quality of Mills' formula. Even grade-schoolers feel comfortable with the observation that every number that is not prime can be expressed as the product of primes in essentially one way. Thus, 630 can be expressed as $2 \cdot 3 \cdot 3 \cdot 5 \cdot 7$, and no other primes will multiply to yield 630. Not only do youngsters believe the result, but it is something that can be readily proven.

In all of our discussion so far, it is worth pointing out that our analysis—be it simple, complicated, surprising, or expected—makes an important assumption about the nature of the particular set we are investigating. It is that number theory in general, and prime number theory in particular, assumes that the set we are interested in exploring is that of N, the *natural numbers*.

Once we make that observation explicit, we open up the possibility of challenging that attribute in a "What-If-Not" spirit. Suppose, for example, that instead of $N = \{1, 2, 3, 4, 5, 6, \ldots\}$ you select the set $E = \{1, 2, 4, 6, 8, 10, \ldots\}$, where E is the set of even numbers together with 1. In this new system, some operations, such as addition, are not closed (that is, when we add two numbers we may "leave" the original set). Other operations are closed, however. For example, when we multiply any two numbers in E, we end up with a number in E. Since E is closed under multiplication, it makes sense to try to develop the concept of prime there. Notice that if we accept the same definition of prime for E that we did for N, then 6 is prime in E, for there are only two divisors of 6 in E. Two cannot divide 6 in E in the same way that 2 cannot divide 5 in N! Remember that although $2 \times 3 = 6$ in N, 3 is not a member of E. You may wish to explore what other numbers are prime in E—and you will be surprised by the regularity of the primes in E.

As you move your focus from N to E, here are three starting points (again, you will find numerous surprises):

1. After defining *even* in E, explore Goldbach's conjecture in that system.
2. In N, we know that every number is either prime or can be represented uniquely as the product of primes. In E, look at several non-primes and see what happens (include 72 as a start), remembering that 5×2 is not an allowable factoring in E, since 5 does not belong to E.
3. *Ulam's Spiral*
   Ulam, a former colleague of Einstein's, was doodling one day and found that if he spiraled the natural numbers as shown in Figure 32, some

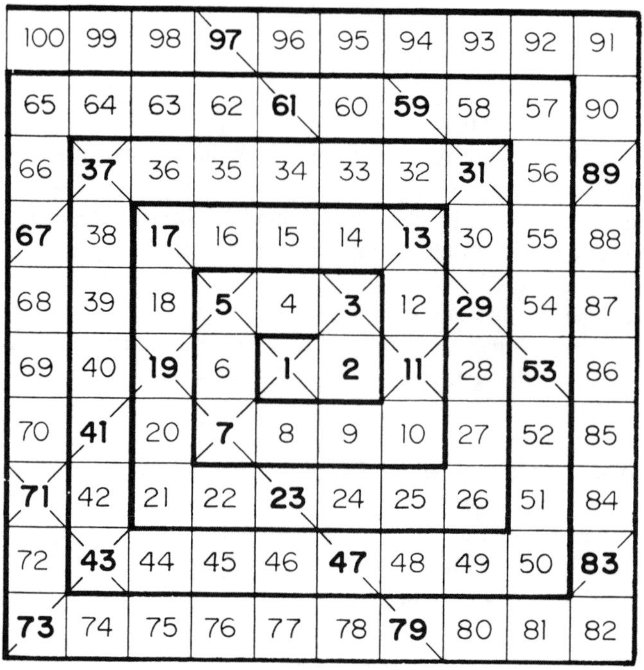

100	99	98	97	96	95	94	93	92	91
65	64	63	62	61	60	59	58	57	90
66	37	36	35	34	33	32	31	56	89
67	38	17	16	15	14	13	30	55	88
68	39	18	5	4	3	12	29	54	87
69	40	19	6	1	2	11	28	53	86
70	41	20	7	8	9	10	27	52	85
71	42	21	22	23	24	25	26	51	84
72	43	44	45	46	47	48	49	50	83
73	74	75	76	77	78	79	80	81	82

FIG. 32.

diagonals are prime-rich and some prime-poor, though none consist only of primes.[21]

Thus, the diagonal with numbers 73, 43, 21, 7, 1, 3, 13, 31, 57, 91 has a relatively large proportion of primes. Compare that diagonal with the numbers along the diagonal 69, 39, 17, 35, 61, 95. Now take the same spiral pattern and fill in the boxes using only elements of E. Investigate the nature of primes along diagonals.

If you begin to explore some of the "What-If-Not" suggestions implied in the investigation of E, you will find that some unsolved problems (unsolved for centuries) in N have solutions so simple in E that they can be produced by a talented junior high school student. This is the case for example with Goldbach's conjecture which you have already explored. If you maintain the same definition of even in E as you do in N (that a number must be divisible by 2 to be even), then the even numbers greater than 2 are 4, 8, 12, 16, 20, ... That is, with the exception of the number 2 only numbers of the form 4n for n belonging to N are

---

[21]See M. L. Stein, S. M. Ulam, and M. B. Wells, "A Visual Display of Some Properties of the Distribution of Primes," *American Mathematical Monthly,* 71 (May 1964), pp. 515–20.

even numbers in E. All other numbers except 1 are prime (why?), and can be expressed as two less than the even numbers in this set. Thus the primes can be expressed as 4n − 2 for n belonging to N. Now, how do you represent any even number greater than 2 (expressible in the form 4n) as the sum of two primes? One obvious way is:

$$4n = (4n - 2) + 2,$$

and a problem that has plagued mathematicians for centuries in N curls up in embarrassment in E!

Thus in exploring the "What-If-Nots" of E derived from N you can gain a better appreciation for the depth of certain properties and characteristics of N. You do even better than that however, for you get a glimpse of a very interesting phenomenon that is more general: You sometimes discover that when you make modifications in something you are investigating, it turns out to have drastically different consequences than you might have anticipated!

"Rational" Behavior[22]

It has become standard fare in algebra courses to take equations and graph them. It is done so unreflectively that we frequently neglect to appreciate the ingenuity of the idea, an ingenuity that harkens back several centuries to the mind of Descartes. The basic notion is that we can establish a correspondence between points in the plane and pairs of real numbers (the coordinates of the points). That correspondence enables us to reduce what appears to be a problem in algebra to one in geometry and vice versa. From this association between points and pairs of numbers we can investigate properties, such as conditions of intersection for straight lines, by interpreting the task as involving the solution of equations.

In that spirit, we reduce information about a given line to an equation of the form y = mx + b, where m is the slope of the line, b is the y intercept and (x,y) represents an arbitrary point. Given the pairs of coordinates for any two points, we can easily come up with the equation for a straight line connecting those points. If we take two such equations for any two lines in the plane, we can find their point of intersection.

All of this leads to results that are expected and somewhat dull. One way to put some life into a dull situation is to explore some of the standard material with an interesting "What-If-Not." Let us, for example focus on the nature of the points we select in the plane. We know, for example, that some numbers (like ⅔, −⅐) are rational numbers, and others (like $\sqrt{2}, \sqrt[3]{7/2}$) are not rational, that is, they cannot be reduced to some number of the form a/b for a and b integers. By looking at the rational/irrational nature of points along a line, we

---

[22]See Stephen I. Brown, "Rationality, Irrationality and Surprise," *Mathematics Teaching,* No. 55, Summer 1971, pp. 13–19.

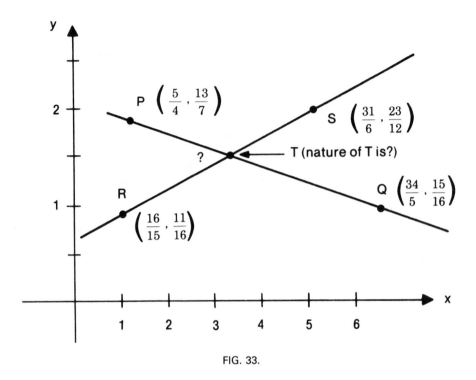

FIG. 33.

find that there is a fascinating and hidden world still to be uncovered even after we know how to locate the intersection points of straight lines, either algebraically or geometrically.

Let us now begin an investigation of straight lines in the plane by focusing on only rational points. Take any two points in the plane, each of which has two rational coordinates. For example, choose $R(^{16}\!/_{15}, \,^{11}\!/_{16})$ and $S(^{31}\!/_{6}, \,^{23}\!/_{12})$. Connect the points with a straight line. Select any other two points both of which have two rational coordinates, for example $P(^{5}\!/_{4}, \,^{13}\!/_{7})$ and $Q(^{34}\!/_{5}, \,^{15}\!/_{16})$ and do the same. Now, calculate the coordinates of the point of intersection T of the two lines and notice the nature of its coordinates. Are both coordinates of T rational? Irrational? Or are they mixed?

From an algebraic point of view, the nature of the coordinates—that they are both rational—is not surprising. Try a few more rational choices for coordinates for points P, Q, R, S. You may wish to prove that for any rational choices of coordinates, the intersection point T will also be rational.

From the point of view of probability theory, however, the conclusion of rationality for the point of intersection is surprising because the probability that the coordinates of a point in the plane *selected at random* will be rational is zero. This suggests that the attribute of rationality associated with each of the coordinates may be more special than we would have guessed. It was the disparity between an algebraic and a probability expectation that accounted for our initial interest in this phenomenon.

Now direct your attention to the attribute of rationality and investigate the implications of some alternatives. We will first need to clarify the concept of rationality and its variation in our investigation. One way to begin would be to define a point as:

- *rational* if both coordinates are rational (as we have done here);
- *irrational* if both coordinates are irrational;
- *semi-rational* otherwise.

As a start, we might consider the concept of rationality (and variations of it) for:

(a) points along a line, or
(b) intersection points of lines.

We might begin our investigation of (a) by asking questions like:

1. Can you have a straight line with only one rational point?
2. Can you have a straight line with only two rational points?
3. Can you have a straight line with only three rational points?
4. How are our answers affected by replacing rational with irrational or semi-rational in the questions above?

After investigating these questions for the lines themselves, look at the nature of (b)—pairs of lines intersecting. Once you appreciate that it is more of a surprise than originally anticipated for *any* two lines, each having two pairs of rational coordinates, to intersect in a rational point, you will have acquired a much more skeptical mind-set with regard to expectations for the case of irrational or semi-rational coordinates.

"Distributing" Things[23]

One of the hallmarks of a modern mathematics program is its focus on the axiomatic nature of a system. Looking, for example, at the natural numbers, we

---

[23]Stephen I. Brown, "Multiplication, Addition and Duality," *Mathematics Teacher*, October 1966, pp. 543–50.

can observe that among the critical properties for addition and multiplication are the commutative and the associative properties. Thus:

$a + b = b + a$; $a \cdot b = b \cdot a$ (commutative properties)

$a + (b + c) = (a + b) + c$; $a \cdot (b \cdot c) = (a \cdot b) \cdot c$
                (associative properties)

There has been a lot of controversy since the early 1960s regarding the value of basing a mathematics program primarily on the axiomatic structure, and recently there has been a resurgence of interest in such areas as application to the real world and to problem solving in general as alternatives.

Although these alternatives are certainly worth taking seriously, one reason a structural approach has received considerable criticism is that it tends to engender a "much ado about nothing" attitude, that is, people find a complicated way of justifying something they believed to be true without all the fanfare. It is often claimed, for example, that every child knows that $5 + 7 = 7 + 5$, regardless of whether or not he or she is aware that the name of the property that justifies it is the commutative property.

It *is* possible, however, to use parts of the structure of mathematics to encourage inquiry that is not a trivialization of axioms already understood in some intuitive sense. Let us choose to do a "What-If-Not" on the distributive property as an illustration. The distributive property asserts algebraically something that is more easily conveyed in the picture of the rectangular region (Figure 34). Notice that the area of the entire rectangle can be gotten by adding the areas of A and B. Thus $a(b + c) = a \cdot b + a \cdot c$. This algebraic statement is referred to as the distributive property, and, like the commutative and associative properties, is something we use intuitively to help us do shortcut calculations. For example, if we calculate 20×32 in our heads by doing $(20 \times 30) + (20 \times 2)$, we are in fact using the distributive property. Among the attributes of that property is the

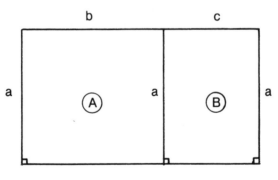

FIG. 34.

observation that unlike the associative and commutative ones, it ties together the two operations of addition and multiplication in one statement.

There are a variety of "What-If-Nots" you can generate based on this observation. Consider one which suggests *switching the roles of the two operations:* What if we did not have a·(b + c) but rather a + (b · c) as our point of entry? Then, an analogy with the traditional distributive property would suggest that a + (b·c) = (a + b)·(a + c), a "dual" of the distributive property, instead of the standard distributive law.

Now a little exploration reveals that this dual distributive property does not hold in general in the set of real numbers (or even in the set of natural numbers for that matter). For example, 2 + (3·7) does not equal (2 + 3)·(2 + 7). But the fact that something *sometimes* fails, does not imply that it *always* fails. If a = 0, it seems pretty straightforward to observe that a + (b·c) = (a + b)·(a + c). Are there any other cases of success?

With only a slight desire to tease, we suggest you try a = ⅓, b = ⅕, c = ⁷⁄₁₅. Check it out. Now what is so special about the triplet ⅓, ⅕, ⁷⁄₁₅ that yields a true instance of the dual of the distributive property? Try adding up the three fractions, and you'll get a clue. Try to state and prove a conjecture based on this observation.

In closing this section, we should point out that an exploration of the disparity in truth value between the original distributive property and its dual has the possibility of leading to some fascinating investigation. If we create a dual by switching addition and multiplication, we notice that both commutative and associative properties have duals that are true, while the distributive property has a dual which fails. It was this observation which first served as a general starting point for our investigating the concept of dual in the set of real numbers. It led to the analysis of a question that you might wish to investigate further, "How can you tell *before* trying to prove any theorem in a system such as that of the real numbers, whether or not it is necessary to invoke the distributive property in the proof?"[24]

Before summarizing the chapter, let us point out that there are several messages embedded in this example that outstrip a particular focus on the distributive property. In investigating the dual, what we have done in a more general way, is to perform a *reversal*. That is, we noticed one attribute of the distributive property. The property links addition with multiplication. Then we *switched* the roles of addition and multiplication, as indicated below:

$$\text{Standard property: } a \cdot (b + c) = (a \cdot b) + (a \cdot c)$$
$$\downarrow \quad \downarrow \qquad \downarrow \quad \downarrow \quad \downarrow$$
$$\text{New property: } \quad a + (b \cdot c) = (a + b) \cdot (a + c)$$

---

[24]For an analysis of this and unexpected finds about the distributive property, see the article cited in footnote 23.

So, we have varied an attribute in a very special way—by interchanging the two operations. After varying the attribute in this special way, we, of course, had another step to perform, as indicated in the "What-If-Not" scheme. That is, we had to *ask a question*. Let us look at what went on in this example in "slow motion" so as to reveal some issues of a more general nature.

Salvaging a Question

When first looking at the new distributive property, our inclination was to ask if it always holds, just as the standard distributive property holds for all numbers. An example chosen at random revealed that it did not always hold. Our first inclination was to move on, rather than to think about further investigation. It took a few seconds, however, to disengage the investigation of the new property from the old, and venture a question about the new one that we never would have asked about the old—namely, "Does it *ever* hold?" We showed by producing one example (a = ⅓, b = ⅕ and c = ⁷⁄₁₅) that it does hold in at least one case and implied that it might hold in others as well.

Further investigation of this observation led to an analysis of the fascinating question we mentioned earlier, "How can you tell *before* proving a theorem (in a field structure) whether or not the distributive property is needed?" A more general question might be, "How can you tell before trying to prove anything in a system whether or not a specific property of the system is needed?" It is not always possible to find the answer for this question, but in those cases in which we can find an answer, we reveal more about the structure of the system than we ever imagined.

There is much embedded in the observation that we modified the question in the new set-up from: "Does the dual of the distributive property always hold?" to "Does it ever hold?"

Recall that earlier we claimed that foolish or nonsensical questions *might* be a hair's breadth away from worthwhile ones. It is also the case, however, that questions are initially meaningful may lead to results that are not too interesting (e.g., that the new distributive property is not always true). A slight modification of a meaningful but dull question, however, can lead to *astounding* results.

Look again at our handy list of questions at the end of chapter 3. Do the questions we have asked about the dual of the distributive property appear there? Perhaps you would like to add new ones suggested by this exploration that do not appear.

The Anatomy of Reversals

Reversal is a kind of "What-If-Not" we performed on the attribute of operations in this example. We just switched addition and multiplication signs and asked some new questions. But there are many ways in which we can try to reverse an attribute or a phenomenon. Let us look at our previous section on prime numbers, for example. There we spoke about Goldbach's conjecture in the set of natural numbers: That any even number greater than two can be expressed as the sum of two primes. In that section, we did a "What-If-Not" on the conjecture to see what happens if we investigate an old question in a new set.

We could, however, not have challenged the *given* set of numbers (changing from the natural numbers to the even numbers together with 1) but rather asked a kind of question again suggested in *Strategy for Phase One Problem generation* in chapter 3. A beautiful pseudo-historical question might be, "How did anyone ever come up with that conjecture?"

If we are doing pseudo-history, we are not concerned about historical accuracy. One conjecture that comes to mind is suggested by a different conception of reversal than we have demonstrated so far. Suppose we look at a *converse* of Goldbach's conjecture: Any two primes added together yield an even number. As it stands the *converse* is false, for if exactly one of the primes is 2, then the sum will be odd. Let us modify the converse slightly, however:

The sum of any two primes (excluding the number 2), is an even number.

That is a true statement if we observe that all primes in N other than 2 are odd numbers, and if we appreciate that the sum of any two odds is an even number. The statement is not only true, but child's play to prove, while Goldbach's conjecture has challenged the best of mathematicians for 250 years!

Now, given the above discussion, how would you guess Goldbach came up with his conjecture? A good pseudo-historical approach would be to suggest that *after* playing with the "trivial" observation that primes added in pairs yield even numbers (well almost always), he may very well have asked himself, "What if I look at the converse?"

So far, then, we have looked at two kinds of reversal: Switching the operations of a statement, and switching the logic of a statement (looking at the converse).

Thus, we have a tool (reversal) for:

1. Modifying attributes.
2. Asking questions.

In a Pulitzer prize-winning book of 1980, Douglas Hofstadter also explores the issue of reversal, but from a slightly different point of view.[25] He locates the roots of creativity in the fields of mathematics, music, and art in a special kind of reversal, the reversal of "figure and ground." He points out how creative work in all these fields frequently depends on *switching* what is in the forefront of

---

[25]Hofstadter, Douglas H., *Gödel, Escher, Bach: An Eternal Golden Braid,* New York: Vintage Books, 1980.

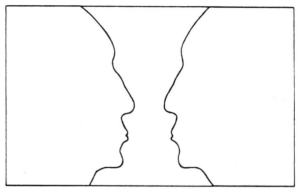

FIG. 35.

investigation with what is in the background. Perceptually, the expression is conveyed by such drawings as Figure 35.

Is it a vase or two people facing each other?

Hofstadter goes on to indicate that Bach fugues were created in a similar vein, and he then points to the roots of some deep metamathematical results (Gödel's theorems) through figure-ground reversal.

So far, then, we have described three different conceptions of reversal. Can you come up with others? Try to use these conceptions of reversal in new applications of the "What-If-Not" scheme.

SUMMARY

In this chapter, we have chosen a diverse set of mathematical ideas as starting points. We have selected concepts from algebra, geometry, number theory and have even had some probability theory sneak its way in. As in chapter 3, we have exemplified a different type of diversity as well. We have used data, a problem, an algorithm and even an activity as points of departure for problem generating. In all of these variations, we have tried to uncover not only a sense of creativity associated with "What-If-Not-ing," but have tried to show how this process frequently enables us to uncover unsuspected depth in starting points that may appear pedestrian. We have done this in part by demonstrating how even apparently slight modifications of a phenomenon frequently have a drastic effect. Problems that have been unsolved for centuries in one context reveal themselves with ease in others (as in the case of Goldbach's conjecture, as well as in many of the other number theory problems). What we take for granted as easy and unsurprising reveals itself as possessing unsuspected depth when subjected to a "What-If-Not" procedure. On the other hand, we have shown that the existence of surprise can act as an invitation to perform a "What-If-Not" in the first place.

In addition, we exhibited throughout this chapter a phenomenon alluded to earlier. That is, we showed how apparently meaningless observations or questions can be significantly rejuvenated through the injection of a "What-If-Not" point of view. In many of the examples here, we made use not only of the "What-If-Not" scheme, but of the problem generating strategies described in chapter 3—strategies such as using pseudo-history, distinguishing between internal and external exploration of phenomena and employing the handy list of questions.

Finally we explored the category of reversals (conceiving of the phenomenon in several different ways) as a way of both modifying attributes and of asking new questions.

6

Some Natural Links Between Problem Posing and Problem Solving

We have been discussing and analyzing problem posing, and in the process, we became involved in problem solving. The two activities are, however, more intimately connected than we have suggested so far. In order to explore their interconnectedness, we begin by looking at one example.

ONE EXAMPLE IN DETAIL

Consider the following problem:

> Given two equilateral triangles, find a third one whose area is equal to the sum of the areas of the other two.

Try to solve it before reading on.

A Beginning

There are many questions you may be asking at this point, such as:

1. We have been provided with neither the lengths nor the areas of the two original triangles. Are we to find the area of the third triangle without that information? What context is assumed and what theorems are relevant?
2. Not only have we not been given specific lengths or areas, but the lengths

or areas of the two triangles have not been denoted by variables. Are we expected to solve this problem algebraically using variables?

3. Since in the preceding problem no numbers are associated with line segments or regions, can we construct the answer purely geometrically?

Before discussing these matters, we should point out that when the kind of information just requested is provided at the outset, our view of the problem may be limited as we are robbed of the opportunity of asking these kinds of questions.

Let us now take each of the queries, in turn, to see how each leads to a different kind of approach, understanding, and insight.

Three Different Analyses

For Those Who Like to Start With Numbers

Consider 3 and 7 as our given lengths. Let us rephrase the problem:

Find the length of the side of an equilateral triangle whose area is equal to the sum of the areas of two equilateral triangles of sides 3 and 7 (Figure 36).

Using the Pythagorean theorem (and assuming h_1, h_2, and h_3 are the three altitudes) we obtain:

$$h_1 = \frac{3\sqrt{3}}{2}, \quad h_2 = \frac{7\sqrt{3}}{2}.$$

Then using the fact that the area of a triangle is one half the length of the base times the altitude, if the areas are A_1, A_2 and A_3:

$$A_1 = \frac{3 \cdot 3\sqrt{3}}{4}$$

$$A_2 = \frac{7 \cdot 7\sqrt{3}}{4}$$

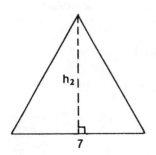
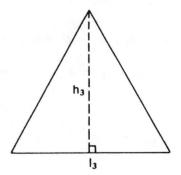

FIG. 36.

$$A_3 = A_1 + A_2 = \frac{\sqrt{3}\,(9 + 49)}{4}$$

$$= \frac{\sqrt{3}\cdot 58}{4} = \frac{29\sqrt{3}}{2}.$$

To find the side l_3 of the required new triangle, using the formula for the area of an equilateral triangle, we might proceed as follows:

$$A_3 = \frac{l_3^2\sqrt{3}}{4} = \frac{29\sqrt{3}}{2}.$$

Therefore,

$$l_3^2 = \frac{29\sqrt{3}}{2}\cdot\frac{4}{\sqrt{3}}$$

$$= 29\cdot 2 = 58;$$

so,

$$l_3 = \sqrt{58}.$$

This solves the problem of finding the length of the required triangle. If we had wanted the area, we could have stopped when we found that:

$$A_3 = \frac{29\sqrt{3}}{2}.$$

Do you have any new insights or new questions at this point? Perhaps you might want to try this example with different numbers, such as 3 and 3, 3 and 4, or 9 and 40 in order to get a feeling for approaching the problem by choosing specific numbers for the lengths of the sides.

This is, of course, just one way of interpreting the problem. Let us now turn to a closely related second method.

For Those Who Prefer to Start With Variables

Find the length t_3 of the side of an equilateral triangle whose area is equal to the sum of the areas of two equilateral triangles of sides t_1 and t_2. (See Figure 37.)

Following the arguments from the previous section, we have

$$A_1 = \frac{t_1^2\sqrt{3}}{4}$$

$$A_2 = \frac{t_2^2\sqrt{3}}{4}$$

$$A_1 + A_2 = \frac{t_1^2\sqrt{3} + t_2^2\sqrt{3}}{4} = A_3 = t_3^2\,\frac{\sqrt{3}}{4};$$

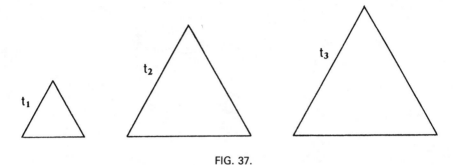

FIG. 37.

therefore $t_3 = \sqrt{t_1{}^2 + t_2{}^2}$. Do you have any further insights at this point?

For Those Who Enjoy Using Segments and Regions

Look back at the two previous approaches. What is suggested by those analyses? If t_1 and t_2 are given line segments, how can we construct line segment t_3? Using a straight edge and compass, we could construct $t_1{}^2$ from t_1, $t_2{}^2$ from t_2, and then $\sqrt{t_1{}^2 + t_2{}^2}$.[1] Notice that unlike the problem of merely adding two line segments, this construction requires the provision of a unit length as well.

However, there is a way out that does not require a unit. Since t_3 is equal to $\sqrt{t_1{}^2 + t_2{}^2}$, we are reminded of the Pythagorean relationship $t_3{}^2 = t_1{}^2 + t_2{}^2$. Therefore, we could have solved the problem as indicated in Figure 38.

---

[1]The construction of $\sqrt{t_1{}^2 + t_2{}^2}$ depends on the two theorems suggested by the pictures below:

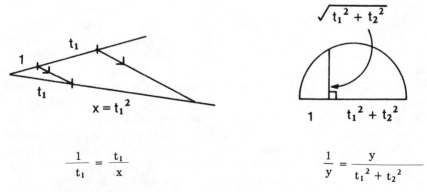

Therefore x is equal to $t_1{}^2$.

First construct $t_1{}^2$ as on the left. Do the same for $t_2{}^2$. Then combine to get $t_1{}^2 + t_2{}^2$, and construct the desired result as indicated by the drawing on the right. Note that a unit length is assumed for both constructions.

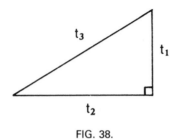

FIG. 38.

Notice that solving the problem this way does not require that we be given t_1 and t_2 relative to a unit length. Despite the elegance of this solution, however, a mystery prevails. Though the algebra suggests this geometric approach, the algebraic link is not particularly illuminating. Is there some essentially geometric rather than algebraic way of seeing directly why we are led to the Pythagorean theorem?

PROBLEM SOLVING YIELDS PROBLEM POSING

Asking "Why"

The question just posed (Is there some essentially geometric way of seeing directly why we are led to the Pythagorean theorem?) suggests that "Why?" is an ambiguous question. The reply that it follows from the *calculation* (since $t_3{}^2 = t_1{}^2 + t_2{}^2$), an answer which is often given, seems at first to be satisfying. However, on further reflection, this reply provides no insight into the situation and, in fact, does not really explain why this result might be expected. The "why" to which we seek an answer here is of a different type; it calls for an explanation that gives us both understanding and insight into the situation. We are suggesting that the solution of our equilateral triangle problem leading us to the Pythagorean theorem may not be an accident of calculation. Rather, it could be the result of deeper connections, connections we are striving to understand more clearly. The connection is not illuminated by merely carrying out the calculation, though of course it was the calculation that made us aware of the connection originally. We are really asking, "Could we have suspected that the solution of our problem would involve the Pythagorean theorem without doing any calculation?" When our conclusions surprise us and we wish to know why they occurred (in the sense of what "caused" the result), a reply which merely retreads the steps of the solution is often not satisfying.

There are other interpretations of "Why?", however. Frequently, when we ask why something is the case in mathematics (after having received some answer), we are really asking, "Is this a special case of a broader generalization or is it a fluke that stands alone?" For instance, if we discover that the medians of a 30°, 60°, 90 ° triangle meet in a point, we might be tempted to ask "Why?", even after we have demonstrated it, to determine if it is a specific instance of a more general case. However, when we find out that $5 + 3 + 13 = 21$ (assuming no further context), we would probably not ask, "Why?" because we would be satisfied that if follows directly from calculation.

As you can see from these few examples, it seems that asking the question, "Why?" can be done on several levels. Let us note that one of the prime problem posing strategies in mathematics—asking why—is more complicated and interesting than appears on the surface.

Now, let us turn to one way of answering "Why?" more specifically, for the conclusion of the problem concerning the construction of an equilateral triangle equal in area to the sum of the areas of two given equilateral triangles.

Answering "Why?"

Background

We have a feeling that the Pythagorean theorem is at the root of this problem. Let us examine it once more. When considered as a geometric statement, the theorem says that the square on the hypotenuse of a right triangle equals the sum of the squares on the other two sides. In a specific example in which two legs are 3 and 4, we can come up empirically with 25 as the area of the square on the hypotenuse by drawing an "accurate" picture (see Figure 39).

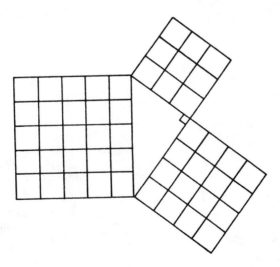

FIG. 39.

How might we gain a deeper understanding of the Pythagorean theorem? Look once more at the statement describing the geometric interpretation of a theorem. What is it talking about? For one thing, it is saying something about the relationship of areas.

Suppose we squint a little and try to find a less literal or a broader interpretation of that relationship. The three figures on the sides are special figures, namely, squares. Instead of drawing only squares on the three sides, what other shapes might we consider? (See Figure 40.)

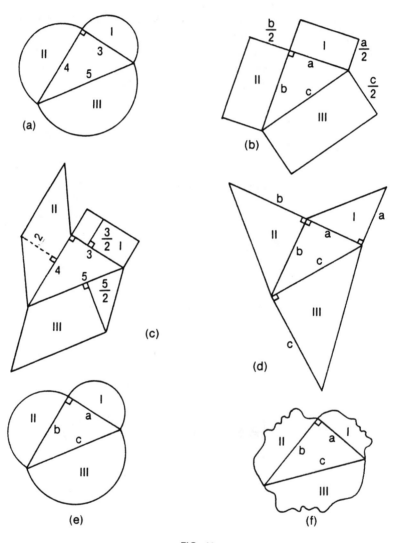

FIG. 40.

If we depict the sides by a, b, c and the areas by I, II, and III, respectively, what relationships might we search for? Holding the Pythagorean theorem in mind, we might be inclined to ask, "Which figures (see Figure 40) have areas that are additive?" (That is, I + II = III.)

For some of the figures it is fairly straightforward to calculate areas of regions drawn on the sides of a right triangle. For example, in Figure 40(a), the three semicircles have area:

$$\frac{\pi(3/2)^2}{2}, \frac{\pi(4/2)^2}{2}, \frac{\pi(5/2)^2}{2},$$

and I + II = III. Look at Figure 40(c)—parallelograms with indicated dimensions. Once more, we get from straightforward calculation that I + II = III.

Examine Figure 40(b), (d), and (e). Although the calculation is also straightforward, we need to make use of the Pythagorean theorem in order to demonstrate additivity, despite the fact that we are no longer dealing with squares on the three sides of the right triangles.

It comes as a real surprise that not only are the areas additive for squares, but they are also additive for sets of other figures. Is there some phenomenon more general than squareness which accounts for additivity? Notice that in all cases but Figure 40(c), the shapes are similar! Can you now rephrase the Pythagorean theorem in a more general form? Although there are many ways of generalizing it, we should like to focus on this conjecture:

> If three similar figures are constructed on three sides of a right triangle, then the areas are additive; that is, the sum of the areas on the legs equals the area on the hypotenuse.

Notice, then, that the Pythagorean theorem itself is a specific example of this conjecture—namely, the special one when the three figures are squares.

Back to the Equilateral Triangle

Now that we have extended our view of the Pythagorean theorem, let us see if it can help us gain insight into the solution of our problem and help us answer why the Pythagorean theorem is involved with a problem dealing with equilateral triangles. If this conjecture is true, then we can finally see why the Pythagorean connection to our original problem for equilateral triangles makes sense. Figure 41 is just an instance of the more generalized Pythagorean theorem, with the similar figures being equilateral triangles. We could therefore solve the original problem by taking the two equilateral triangles and placing their sides at right angles with a common vertex. Thus, by drawing an equilateral triangle on the hypotenuse, we obtain an equilateral triangle equal in area to the sum of the other two!

Notice that here we have an elegant solution to our original problem (finding

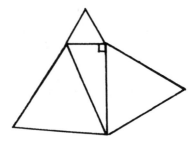

FIG. 41.

an equilateral triangle equal in area to the sum of the areas of the two given equilateral triangles). The solution is elegant because it is simple, unexpected and requires that only the sides of the equilateral triangle be given rather than the *lengths* of the sides or the areas of the original triangles. We have thus answered "Why?" in a way that places the problem in a broader perspective than if we had merely calculated to find $t_3 = \sqrt{t_1^2 + t_2^2}$. [2]

REFLECTIONS ON NATURAL LINKS

"The After Effect"

There are a number of interesting problem posing issues beneath the surface in the previous example. First, we allowed ourselves and encouraged you to explore a problem that was *vaguely* defined. We did not stipulate at the beginning whether numbers (lengths or area) were to be associated with the equilateral triangles or segments or regions. We did not specify whether we were looking for algebraic or geometric solutions, nor did we indicate the geometric tools of analysis that were to be considered relevant.

We may well be robbed of a great deal of serious thinking by insisting on clarity at early stages in the definition of problems. It is worthwhile to investigate all the different ways in which "the given" can be interpreted, as well as how the analysis might depend on the different assumptions and tools we allow ourselves to use. In fact, we frequently prevent ourselves from seeing that the clarification of a problem is itself a significant intellectual task. It can lead to

---

[2]For further development of the ideas described in this section, see George Polya, *Mathematics and Plausible Reasoning,* Princeton, N.J.: Princeton University Press, 1954, Vol. 1 (pp. 15–17), and Marion Walter and Steven Brown, "Problem Posing and Problem Solving: an Illustration of Their Interdependence," *Mathematics Teacher,* Vol. 70, No. 1, Jan. 1977, pp. 4–13. Much of the analysis in the latter piece was inspired by the aforementioned section of Polya's book, in which he offers a brilliant analysis of the relationships among generalization, specialization and analogy in mathematical thought.

posing and solving many interesting problems along the way, as well as to a deeper understanding of what is involved. Unfortunately, many of us equate "clearly stated" with "good" in the posing of problems.

The second problem posing issue we have suggested is that it is worth asking "Why?" with many different intentions; that is, some "whys" call for calculation, some for insight into a gestalt, some for a broader generalization.

But there is a third point embedded here which is even more critical for the purpose of exposing natural links between problem posing and problem solving: It is *after* we have supposedly solved a problem that we are pressed to ask some new questions. It is because we are surprised, puzzled or confused by an approach we have taken or a conclusion we have reached, that we feel compelled to ask a new set of questions. Indeed, why *do* the areas of equilateral triangles add up on the sides of a right triangle the way the squares do in the Pythagorean theorem?

In the previous section of this chapter, we jumped rather quickly to the hunch that perhaps the shared property of similarity among the three polygons (for equilateral triangles and squares) accounted for the unexpected conclusion. You could, of course, explore other first hunches for why the areas are additive. Perhaps the fact that the polygons are regular (equilateral and equiangular) might account for the result, or could it be that there is some other explanation?

Our main point here is that frequently *after* we have solved a problem we are in a position to pose a new set of questions.

We now have both a logical observation that connects problem solving with problem posing and a new problem generating heuristic: Take an alleged proof which either surprises you or which lacks illumination as an opportunity to generate new sets of questions.

Here is another example to illustrate the point. In chapter 4, we alluded to the Gauss example for finding the sum of the numbers from 1 to 100. We suggested a strategy for solving, namely to observe that if properly perceived, we really had many pairs of numbers with sums of 101. In this way we can get the solution to the original problem. However, most people who see this approach are prompted to ask a number of new questions because they are still puzzled. Looking back, do you find yourself dissatisfied? If so, what questions does your discomfort spark in you?

Here are some questions that we have found others asking after they had been shown the Gauss solution and after they had played around with the problem for a while:

1. How did anyone even come up with this approach?
2. Suppose the last number in the original sum were not 100, but some other number. Would it still work?
3. Is there something special about the fact that the last number is even? What would happen if the sum ended at 99 instead of 100?

4. Is there some general formula that captures this clever observation?
5. To what extent can I capture the overall, general situation in this specific observation?

There are of course many other questions that you might ask here. We should clarify that here we are not trying to generate new questions, as we did when we were "What-If-Not-ing"; rather, we are trying to generate questions with a specific goal in mind—namely, to help us understand *why* a particular conclusion, that has supposedly been proven, is meaningful.

The "Prior Effect"

There is a second natural link between problem posing and problem solving— one in which the temporal order just described is reversed. That is, we need not wait until *after* we have solved a problem to generate new questions; rather, we are logically obligated to generate a new question or pose a new problem in order to be able to solve a problem *in the first place*.

We will illustrate this point with another problem that we would like you to analyze. First look at the problem, and then write down, as accurately as you can, all of the ideas that occur to you as you try to solve it in the next 10 minutes:

A fly and train are 15 km apart. The train travels towards the fly at a rate of 3 km/hr. The fly travels towards the train at a rate of 7 km/hr. After hitting the train, it heads back to its starting point. After hitting the starting point, it once more heads back toward the train until they meet. The process continues. What is the total distance this fly travels?

With some insight, it is possible to solve the problem with almost no machinery, despite the fact that it first may appear to be a problem involving an infinite geometric progression. What is that insight?

It is clear from the question that we are being asked to focus on the fly. That is the object whose distance we wish to calculate. Yet a brief disengagement from our focus which directs our attention (even momentarily) to the train, has the potential of unleashing some powerful insights. If we ask, "How far does the train travel?" then the problem becomes easier to analyze. We were given this information in the problem. Having asked that new question which redirects our perspective on the problem, it takes only a small leap to ask, "How long does it take the train to travel that distance?"

With some additional visual imagery, we might reach the conclusion that the *time* of travel is the same for both objects. This observation essentially unlocks the problem.

Now there are many ways of gaining insight on this problem, and you need not necessarily follow the chain of thinking just outlined. What we *are* claiming, however, is that something tantamount to the generation of some new question(s) is part of the problem solving act.

Before turning to a less fanciful example, we would like to pass on a delightful story told about this problem. John Von Neumann (1903–1957) was a Hungarian mathematician who emigrated to the United States in 1930. The founder of game theory and other important mathematical topics, he was capable of calculating in his head at a speed that compared favorably with the computers of his day. When a friend gave him the fly/train problem, he got the answer in less than a second. When his friend congratulated him on his solution, telling Von Neumann that most people try to get the answer by finding the sum of an infinite progression—a quite time consuming task—Von Neumann responded, "Is there any other way to do it"?

A More Mundane Example

The Art of Problem Posing came close to reaching a disastrous fate as we argued over the inclusion of the preceding example. One of us wanted to delete the previous subsection because the example seemed too "slick" for the point being made. Finally, we decided to keep the point but to test it against a more mundane example, an example that everyone had learned, like the quadratic formula. Does our problem generation "prior effect" point still hold? Here goes:

Suppose you have the equation $ax^2 + bx + c = 0$ and want to derive the "quadratic formula."

We know how to solve some quadratics by factoring, but not all. How can we proceed? We know that when we solve linear equations, we isolate variables on one side and the constants on the other. So let us write:

$$(i) \quad ax^2 + bx = -c$$

It is a start which, by the way, requires no new question asking for most people. Now what? Anyone seeing this problem for the first time, and who has some background and wants to solve it, might procede by observing, "I know how to solve linear equations, *some* quadratics by factoring and even some equations of higher degree (each of which you know how to solve) like:

$$(ii) \quad d{\cdot}y + e = f;$$
$$y^2 = k;$$
$$(gy + h)(py + q) = 0;$$
$$y^n = m,$$

where y is a variable and the other letters are constants. How can I view (i) so that it is like something in (ii)?"

Ah! Here, finally, is the problem generation heuristic needed to solve this problem. If you have never solved (i) before by putting it into one of the forms of (ii), we encourage you to try to do so now!

We shall not go through the details at this point, and it certainly takes additional insight to "complete the square" (one way of solving the problem) of (i), but such completion must begin with something like the new question we have just asked.

Now let us go one step further and see what we can find out by trying to solve a special case rather than the general quadratic equation.

Consider:

$$x^2 + x - 1 = 0.$$

Let us *challenge* rather than *accept* some well-entrenched method of solving equations. We will be searching for an alternative to completing the square, as well as to collecting unknowns on the same side of the equation. Thus we will employ a "What-If-Not" approach on standard procedures that are frequently unquestioned.

1. Let us start by splitting up the x's:
$$x^2 - 1 = -x,$$
2. Then $(x + 1) \cdot (x - 1) = -x$ by factoring,
3. Then
$$x - 1 = \frac{-x}{x + 1}$$
by division,
4. $x = 1 - \dfrac{x}{1 + x} = \dfrac{1 + x - x}{1 + x} = \dfrac{1}{1 + x}.$

Well, we have what we asked for. We split up the x's in step (1)—an unconventional approach—but we have not gotten anywhere because they are still split in step (4)

$$x = \frac{1}{1 + x}.$$

Nevertheless, continue by replacing the x on the right-hand side by

$$\frac{1}{1 + x}$$

since

$$x = \frac{1}{1 + x}.$$

Thus, $\dfrac{1}{1 + x}$ transforms to $\dfrac{1}{1 + \boxed{\dfrac{1}{1 + x}}}$.

But don't stop here; replace x again by $\dfrac{1}{1 + x}$

$$x = \cfrac{1}{1 + \cfrac{1}{1 + \cfrac{1}{\boxed{\dfrac{1}{1 + x}}}}}$$

What would you estimate the expression on the right to be? How would you calculate it? Compare it to what you get when you use the quadratic formula in this special case.[3]

Our apologies for teasing you in this last example! We obviously did not apply the well-known equation-solving strategies here. Quite the contrary, we solved this problem by *violating* one of the most fundamental rules of equation solving; we split up the unknowns on both sides of the equation. Of course this all was a digression, from the main point of indicating how problem generation is a necessary condition for problem solving. It was a useful digression, however, for we have once more been able to show the power of "What-If-Not" thinking. We negated the attribute which says, "The solution of equations in general requires that we collect all of the unknowns on one side and the constants on the other."

This digression, while not the main point, is not so far from the mark of this reflection section, however. For now that you realize (or are coming to realize) that you *can* solve this quadratic equation with this method, you probably are stimulated to ask a number of new questions, such as, "What's so special about using the *splitting unknowns* procedure on *this* particular quadratic? Can we use it on others? on all?"

But that takes us right back to the first portion of this reflection section, to the after effect, in which we discussed how it is that we did not appreciate our solution to a problem until we had begun to ask and analyze a new *why* question that went beyond the desire to calculate the original answer.

---

[3]If you are puzzled as to how to calculate, just "top off or eliminate" succeeding parts of the continued fraction just as you would do if you have to approximate .3333 . . . Thus calculate, in turn,

$$\frac{1}{1} \, , \quad \cfrac{1}{1 + \cfrac{1}{1}} \, , \quad \cfrac{1}{1 + \cfrac{1}{1 + 1}} .$$

SUMMARY

In earlier chapters of this book, we have argued for the value of problem generation apart from its intimate and immediate relationship to problem solving. In addition, we have suggested specific strategies for such activity. In this chapter, however, we have been less concerned with specific strategies for problem posing and more interested in exhibiting a strong connection between problem posing and problem solving. We have shown, first of all, that frequently we do not appreciate the significance of an alleged solution without generating and analyzing further problems or questions. Secondly, we have claimed that the act of problem solving requires some reformulation of the original problem that is essentially a problem generating activity.

7

In the Classroom: Student as Author and Critic

How might one teach a course that makes use of the problem-generating ideas we have developed in this book? There are certainly many possibilities, but we would like to suggest the bare outline of one scheme we developed over a period of several years. Though there are several features of our course, the central conception is that of *student as author and as editorial board member*. Placing the student in such a role is a radical notion because it assumes a kind of expertise normally reserved for professionals. Such a reversal of role however is consistent with our fundamental notion that students ought to participate actively in their own education and not be mere recipients of knowledge.

Our students, for the most part, are undergraduate or beginning graduate students in the field of mathematics education—although, as we indicated in the introduction, several of them have come from fields as diverse as anthropology, law, and history. As will become apparent as you view descriptions of some of the journal articles produced, very little in the way of technical knowledge was required, although it was assumed that the students had acquired some degree of appreciation for the nature of mathematical thinking.

COURSE DESCRIPTION

As a start, we will reproduce a catalogue description of our course:

Generating and Solving Problems in Mathematics

The main purpose of this course is to provide a context which will counteract an approach to mathematics which is characterized by clear organization of content, clearly posed problems, logical development of definitions, theorems, proofs. We intend instead to provide students with some feeling for mathematics-in-the-making. We will engage in and explore techniques for generating problems, solving problems, providing structure for a mass of disorganized data, reflecting on the processes used in the above activities, analyzing moments of insight, analyzing "abortive" attempts.

The main structural feature of the course, which provides a focus for other activities, is the creation of several journals—physical entities, each of which is created by groups of students throughout the semester, final drafts of which are produced for all members of the class by the end of the course.

To create the journal, the class is divided into several editorial boards (with three to five members on a board). Throughout the semester students write papers which they submit to boards other than their own. Each board offers written criticism to authors and passes judgment on the papers submitted. They decide to accept, reject or require revisions of student papers. After they have had some practice in criticizing papers, each board begins to establish a policy indicating what kind of material and what writing style it most admires. Once a policy is established, each board publicizes it so that students can decide to submit to a board that is most sympathetic with their point of view.

Sources for journal articles include:

1. Problems or situations arising out of class discussions.
2. Problems or situations suggested by instructors every so often.
3. Articles on problems appearing in professional journals.

The papers can be a student's first attempt at defining, analyzing, or solving a problem. The students can also extend, solve, analyze, criticize one of the topics previously dealt with in the course. We stress that if a problem is selected as a starting point it is not necessary that it be solved. Papers include discussions of false starts, introspection on insights or misconceptions, and a list of related topics and specific problems generated while solving the original problem.

Not only are attempts (even unsuccessful ones) to solve problems valued, but other activities not strictly related to solutions at all are considered worthwhile. On some occasions, for example, students decided to write about their efforts to understand the significance of a problem. Some even decide to write about what they imagined the history of the problem might have been.

Besides the articles themselves, the journals include:

- An abstract for each accepted article.
- Letters of acceptance (or required revisions) sent to the author. (Sometimes the original draft, a letter requiring revision and the final draft all appear in the journal. They indicate the kind of reflection encouraged among students.)

- A list of interesting problems that come up in class or in small group or editorial board discussions.
- A list of books or articles either related to specific problems that have been explored or that provide general background for topics or articles.

In addition to responding to the instructor's call for papers, each board is encouraged to initiate a call for papers that reflects its own emerging policy. Some boards have requested criticism and evaluation of the course: others have called for additional problem posing strategies beyond those discussed in class; still others have run contests for the most interesting pedagogical or mathematical problem students have experienced.

ORGANIZATION OF THE COURSE

Phase 1: Pre-journal Writing

The style and content of the course change as the term progresses. In the first phase of the course the instructor usually selects topics that are rich as a potential source for solving problems. Though some problem posing is encouraged, the primary focus at the beginning of this phase is on solving problems individually, in small groups, and in a large group discussion.

In order to enable students to become aware of different approaches to problem solving among their peers, we occasionally pair students and have them observe each other's effort at working on a problem. They take notes on strategies used and we discuss the different styles exhibited. We attempt to maintain a descriptive rather than a judgmental tone, for we are not so much trying to teach a "right way" of approaching problems, as we are hoping to make people sensitive to what they actually do. If it does not appear to interfere unduly with their activity, students (especially when they are paired up to listen to each other) think out loud during problem solving in order to aid in a diagnosis of their style of approach. In order to gain a clearer picture of the problem solving strategy used, it is helpful at this stage to give the students problems that require some manipulation of materials rather than pencil and paper alone. The geoboard is a good source of problems for this purpose; so are problems involving objects like toothpicks and discs. The famous Tower-of-Hanoi puzzle (moving discs of different diameters from one spindle to another according to certain rules) is a good one to use. So are ones like the cherry-in-the-glass problem as described below:

Four toothpicks enclose a cherry. What is the minimum number of picks you can move so that the cherry is outside the "glass"?

Phase 2: Beginning Journal Activity

After students have begun to become familiar with different approaches to problem solving with their peers, we introduce some readings that (a) describe heuristics of problem solving, (b) distinguish styles of thinking and problem solving, and (c) suggest "blocks" to the activity, as well. We continue to assign readings throughout the rest of the course, but neither in this phase nor in later ones do we have a pre-established set of readings. Although the three categories just described are usually represented, selections are made based on the interest and mood of the students. Many of the readings are selected from the bibliography of this text.

Among "classics" that we have found useful for such exploration are those by Adams (on blocks to problem solving), Polya (on heuristics), and Ewing (on styles of problem solving). We should stress, however, that these are all popular categories in mathematics education and in psychology as well, and there is a growing body of literature that is both expanding and refining issues in each of these areas. Anyone teaching a course of this sort would most likely receive considerable help by reviewing recent issues of professional journals in mathematics education and psychology, and by consulting with colleagues in related fields as well.

Gradually, we begin to encourage students to pose problems based on the ones they have attempted to solve, but at this stage no explicit problem generating strategies are discussed. At this stage, too, we encourage students to record their attempted solutions, insights and newly generated problems, although no official journal activity is introduced.

After about three or four class sessions, we encourage students to state explicitly some of the problem-posing techniques they have used implicitly in the first phase of the course. At this stage we begin to formalize some of the strategies we have developed in chapters 3 and 4 of the text. During this second stage, students begin the journal activity. We introduce them to new problems as potential starting points for their articles, and also encourage them to return to the problems they worked on during the first phase—this time armed with some explicit strategies for generating new problems from what was perceived to be "milked dry."

Among the criteria we have used to select mathematical topics for the first two phases of the course are the following:

1. All students should have some machinery available to define and attack problems in the area. Some might make use of special cases and diagrams; others might deal more abstractly with the topic.
2. Topics should lend themselves to examination from a number of different perspectives (e.g. algebraic, geometric, number theoretic points of view).
3. Although innocent looking on the surface, topics should have unsuspected depth.

4. Problems should be such that students can be enticed by easily suggested "situations" that require a relatively small amount of formal definition.

What satisfies the criteria just listed depends on the background and sophistication of the students. One could select from an endless number of topics or situations that would both meet the criteria and satisfy the appetites of students ranging from those in elementary school to those doing doctoral work. Many of the topics discussed earlier in this book have made excellent points of departure for journal writing among our students.

Phase 3: The Journal in Full Bloom

Once students begin to feel comfortable writing articles and receiving criticism from their peers (usually after the first round) we move into the third phase of the course, in which we select content based on specific interests of students and encourage them to *collaborate* not only in their thinking about problems but in their writing as well. We also have them begin to reflect (in journal articles) on their idiosyncratic styles of thinking. Since students have not done very much in the way of collaboration before, it is helpful to indicate to them how use of different perspectives and reflection upon different experiences might enrich the task of writing up a group paper.

The following is a typical group-written assignment:

Choose a question or observation related to Pythagorean triples and work on it in a small group for a while. For next week each member of the group should focus (in three pages or so) on a different question of the sort indicated below:

1. What did you find out mathematically?
2. What were some of the problem solving strategies that were used?
3. What things that you tried as a group were abortive?
4. How does the group problem solving strategy in this case compare with your problem solving strategies in others?
5. What other problems came up or were created when you worked in this group?
6. What were your emotional reactions? What turned you on? Off?
7. What were the different roles played by people in the group?
8. Other?

We believe it is important for students to reflect on how their styles of thinking affect their ability to work in collaboration with others, and also to see how they perform as a function of who initiates the task they work on. Thus, we encourage students to work at least once in each of the following four conditions, and to reflect in writing (for at least one paper) on the difference in their performance under these varying circumstances.

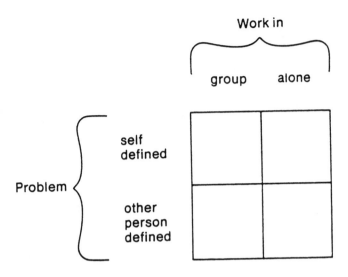

Once the students have reached this phase of the course, they are prepared to put into action some of the board-initiated activity we described earlier (such as a call for papers on topics of their own choosing).

A WORD OF CAUTION

It is worth stressing that, despite an air of excitement and commitment, we sometimes reach a point of discomfort (usually about one-third of the way through the course or just prior to the requirement that an article be submitted, whichever occurs first) among several of our students. Some students are very concerned about submitting a paper to be evaluated by an editorial board comprised of peers in light of the fact that abortive as well as valuable efforts are disclosed, and in which no final solution of a problem is necessarily expected.

Some students are especially concerned about "airing their dirty linen" in public, especially if they have an image of mathematics as "polished" and "impersonal." We have found it to be both essential and valuable to allow students' discontent to surface and especially to encourage discussion among class members over the issues involved. We have found it worthwhile to encourage students to submit an article to one of the class journals in which they try to explore those very issues. The experience of the course is a threatening one, in part because students' prior mathematical experience has taught them to operate in a relatively passive and receptive mode, and to do so non-collaboratively.

It will be necessary, therefore, for teachers who wish to adopt this model to consider different methods of easing students into the role of author and critic.

The manner and degree of acclimatization will depend on such factors as age, intellectual sophistication and ability of students to handle peer criticism.

It is important for instructors of such a course to find ways of allaying some of the aforementioned fears that students may have in order to pave the way for significant growth. In order to encourage them to take the kinds of risk we have described, we have found it helpful to assume a grading policy which offers a number of different opportunities to display their many talents. The following is an excerpt of a memo of ours from a recent adventure in teaching a problem posing course to graduate students in mathematics education.

Grading

Since we want to encourage you to (1) reflect upon your abortive as well as successful efforts in thinking about problems, (2) express your feelings (in writing and orally) about your work on activities associated with the course and (3) accept in a non-threatened way the evaluation of your colleagues, it would be unusual indeed for students who attend the class regularly and who participate in good faith with the class requirements to receive a grade that is not satisfactory.

There will be no examinations or traditional type terms papers submitted at the end of the semester. The grade for each student will depend upon:

1. participation in class discussions and group work.
2. participation as a member of an editorial board (judged by both the process of producing a journal and by the final product).
3. the quality of the articles produced for the editorial boards.

While the instructors will determine that portion of the grade associated with (1) and (2) above, there will be heavy reliance upon the judgment of fellow editorial board members for (3). A student who has pursued the writing of journal papers seriously but has not had a stellar reception by the boards might still receive a good grade based upon performance in the other activities in the course. In addition, though the instructors do not wish to compete with the editorial board judgments during the course of the semester, they will be happy to render independent judgment on the quality of your submitted papers at the end of the semester should you feel that you have not received a fair hearing by your peers.

Regardless of its relationship to grading, however, the role of critic is difficult for many students to assume without first discussing the matter explicitly. Students may wish to discuss both the *value* (and potential pitfalls as well) of criticizing the work of peers, and potential criteria to be used in such criticism. With some encouragement, we find that most students find good reasons for either replacing or supplementing the critical, judgmental, and helpful role normally assumed by the teacher as authority. They come to appreciate that their colleagues may have a refreshingly open and sympathetic reaction to their efforts in approaching new and somewhat risky tasks. In addition, they frequently see their role of critic as one which has considerable potential to be turned "inward" for the purpose of improving their own writing as well.

Once they are persuaded of the value of peer criticism, the editorial boards may need help in coming up with an interesting and coherent editorial board policy. Towards this end, we have found it helpful to have discussions that center on the creation of relevant categories even before positive or negative valences are placed on them. An example of such a category might be "style of exposition." Some boards will eventually select those papers that appear to be tightly argued in a way that may resemble familiar expositions. Others will prize papers that are more chatty in tone. Other "neutral" categories that students have found helpful for the purpose of beginning to think about the nature of their criticism are: relationship of problem posing to problem solving; creation of new territory versus reflection upon mathematical ideas with which the student has been familiar for a while; "heaviness of tone" (including, for example the place of humor desired in the paper); degree of succinctness. There are many others that instructors and students will come up with in conversations over several weeks, but the important point we wish to stress at this point is that it is helpful to discuss categories at early stages that appear relevant but at the same time are not "preachy" or value-laden.

Each teacher will have to find a way of modifying the rough scheme we are presenting. In fact, we urge teachers who want to make use of our editorial board strategy to do a "What-If-Not" on the scheme itself—depending on the specific circumstances of the students they teach, as well as their particular goals for teaching. We encourage teachers who are using our approach to adopt such an attitude, despite the sense of insecurity that may accompany it, for we believe not only that problem posing and problem solving are important activities for mathematics students, but that the teaching act itself ought to be viewed in a problematic way. In fact, we fear that despite a new interest in problem solving in the mathematics curriculum, many educators will try erroneously to persuade teachers that a particular package or program will guarantee success. We believe that teaching anything ought to be viewed as problematic, and this implies that no topic (especially not problem posing and problem solving) and no teaching approach should be viewed as something to be "bought" on someone else's say-so. In fact, we believe that all of us ought to be plagued regularly by questions like:

- Why is problem solving being pushed as a central curriculum theme?
- Why should it be taught?

- How does problem solving fit in with other things that are important to learn?

An advantage of adopting a problematic and "What-If-Not" attitude towards our proposed scheme is that it may become accessible not only to mathematics teachers who wish to focus on areas other than problem posing, but to teachers of other disciplines as well.

"SNIPPETS" OF JOURNAL MATERIALS

Keeping in mind the disclaimer of the last section, it might be helpful to see some actual examples of material produced by our students for the journal. The following are illustrations of editorial policy, letters to authors of articles, typical tables of contents for a complete journal, and excerpts from "published" articles.

Editorial Board Policy Statements

In order to gain some feeling for the diversity of editorial policies developed by students when they are given free rein, we reproduce the following two statements from the journals entitled *Looking Inside a Problem* and *Converging Corners, Diverging Directions*.

I. Looking Inside a Problem

"Contents: The board will accept articles on any topic that is interesting for the class and brings forth personal contributions. We would particularly like to receive articles that express your own thinking and feelings.

Form: In order to be published, the article must be clear, interestingly and well written. There is no restriction on length.

Revisions: Revisions will be concerned with the form of the article. We will only suggest modifications in the content:

—when the writer has added something new to an argument already produced in class that would be worth adding to the article

—if there is an overlap between two articles which we would like to accept; we may ask one of the two to re-write his/her article. We feel this will avoid too much repetition.

We will be happy to discuss any of the suggested revisions if you feel it is necessary. We would like, in some cases, to have the right to summarize a collection of articles on a similar topic rather than publishing each of them independently."

II. Converging Corners, Diverging Directions

"Our board is looking more for papers with some insight into the thinking process than for original solutions and problems. We do appreciate successful solutions and unusual problems in topics like number theory or geometry; however, we would prefer a paper that did not find a clear 'answer' but was rich in discussion of the problem-solving and problem-posing styles. This is preferred to a straightforward proof.

We are looking for papers that deal with issues such as style of problem solving, abortive efforts, how you were able to make certain insights, and other problems you generated. We add to this some related questions. Do you see points in your paper where you could have used another method? Why did you choose the method you did? How did the wording of the question affect your style? How can your solution be applied to real-life situations in or out of the classroom? How can your insights to your problem-solving and problem-posing style be applied? We could go on indefinitely.

We urge you to keep your scratch work and to be constantly aware of your thought pattern. Observe yourself while you are working. Ask yourself why you decided to do what you are doing. In math courses, we are trained to include only the 'correct' answer. Please analyze and include some of your mistakes or dead-end ideas. There are several reasons for this. Is it an error that you make repeatedly? Were you quick to recognize an error or did you make a series of assumptions based on your mistake? Maybe it wasn't really an error or a dead-end. Someone else might pick it up.

We will not automatically exclude any paper that does not deal directly with aspects we have brought up. We will consider each submitted paper on its own merits. Our policies are not exclusive. . . .

In summary, we are more interested in the means than in the end. We do enjoy a well thought out solution, especially if we get some insights into how minds work. A 'failure' at reaching a solution of a problem may be as fruitful a vehicle for discussion as a success. Finally, we read your papers with an open mind."

Letters to Authors

Not only do we encourage editorial boards to indicate in writing why they decide to reject articles, but we also have them provide reasons for acceptance. The following are three examples of letters of acceptance, in two cases with requests for minor revisions:

"Dear Mr. P,

We accepted your paper because
(1)   your procedure was well defined

(2)   your work was readable

(3)   you showed imagination in your varied approaches.

We do, however, recommend several improvements for your future submissions. We ask for more analysis into your thought process by asking that you:

(1)   explain in more detail why you abandoned certain approaches

(2)   explain in more detail how you drew your conclusions.

This paper is concerned with various approaches in finding nonintegral rational solutions (x,y) for the equation $x^2 + y^2 = 25$. While it does not provide solutions it very nicely illustrates strategies of problem solving.

Sincerely,
The Phantom Board"

"Dear Ms. B,

After careful consideration, we are pleased to inform you of our decision to accept your paper for publication. We hope you will continue to submit your papers to our journal in the future.

The points of your article that convinced us to accept your work are your narrative style and your inclusion of the various attempts in solving the problem. The strongest point, we feel, is the paragraphs on similarities and differences of your and Mr. R's approach to the problem, including your comments on pressure and time restrictions.

We would like to suggest a few slight revisions before publication. Please clarify the listings on the last page, possibly combining #3 and #6 into the same statement and especially your statement #5 which we feel is difficult to understand. Also, on page two, please reword the first sentence and place the diagram apart from the narrative.

Again, we congratulate you on this fine article.

Sincerely,
Jay Cubed Enterprise"

"Dear Miss J,

We are writing this letter to congratulate you on the acceptance of your paper, "Observations on the Fly-Train Problem," in our most distinguished journal. The fine qualities of the paper, such as your own personal touches, your conversational style of writing, and the contrast between your approach and that of your partner, all add to the excellence of your paper.

There are several ideas we thought you may want to revise or add to . . .

In your paper, you discussed different approaches to problem solving. You mentioned particularly the abstract approach of the problem solver, in contrast to your own pencil and paper approach. We would be interested in finding out why you feel that the abstract approach is more beneficial to a problem solver.

Do you believe it is always better? If so, can we develop or teach thinking in the abstract?

These are just a few questions you may want to deal with in your next paper.

With Curiosity,
NARC''

Typical Tables of Contents

Here are two tables of contents. Notice that the first entry of the first journal includes both the original submission and the revised one based upon criticism made by the board. Notice also that some of the articles reflect on the problem posing and problem solving processes themselves. In each case, board members have prepared brief ''blurbs'' for accepted articles.

We have attempted to maintain the format and descriptions that appeared in the actual journals. Some of these topics may appear to be somewhat cryptic out of context, but it should be possible to gain an overall flavor for the kinds of topics that were explored and the kind of spirit engendered in the students' writing as you peruse the following annotated tables of contents. It is of course necessary to appreciate that each group of students puts its own distinctive mark on the content and style of the journal.

1. Table of Contents of Board π

GEOBOARD INSPIRED

> *Squares on the Geoboard,* Mr. W_1
> - Original paper
> - Critique by Mr. J_1
> - Revision of the original
>   How many different squares are there on an n $\times$ n geoboard?

> *Back to the Geoboard,* Mr. R_1
>   Counting all possible squares on an n $\times$ n geoboard.

The Orchard Problem, Mr. A_1, Mr. A_2, Ms. C_2, Mr. W_1
How can we tell if a particular tree is see-able in an infinite orchard?

Circles on the Geoboard, Ms. K_2
How many nails are on or inside the largest circle that fits within the geoboard? Relationships of the form $a^2 + b^2 = c^2 + k$ are investigated and some surprising relationships are found.

The Rainy Day Seedlings Problem, Ms. C_1
An approximation of π via the geoboard.

Envelopes of Lines on the Geoboard, Mr. R_1
Constructing envelopes on the geoboard.

An Area Problem, Ms. K_2
Determining the area of a diamond figure that does not have a peg at each vertex on a 5×5 geoboard.

MATHEMATICAL GAMES

Lucks and Bagels, Mr. R_2
Mathematics in disguise.

CIRCLES AND QUADRILATERALS

Quadrilaterals Tangent to Two Circles, Mr. C_2
What is the smallest and largest quadrilateral in which two tangent circles can be inscribed?

Geometry and Calculus Recalled, Mr. F_1
An excursion abounding with errors and incompletion which might be the basis for critical analysis.

MOTIONS IN THE PLANE

Tessellations, Mr. R_1
Any quadrilateral tessellates the plane.

Chocolate Chip Geometry, Mr. R_1 and Ms. W_1
Rotating the plane about particular points.

Translations, Rotations, and Flips in the Plane, Ms. C and Ms. W_1
Exploring rigid motions of a figure in the plane.

Messing Around with Math, Ms. A_1
Motions through matrices.

MIN-MAX TOPICS

The Bridge Problem, Ms. A_2
The use of paper folding in finding minimum paths.

Points, Lines, and Distances, Ms. W_2
Explores minimum paths between points and lines.

Reflections on Polygons, Ms. C_1
Shortest paths within a polygon.

POLYGONS

Shortest Paths and Shortest Paths in 3-Dimensions, Mr. S_1, Ms. C, Ms. W_2
An analysis of shortest paths through reflections.

Construction of Polygons, Given the Midpoints of the Sides, Ms. A_2, Ms. A_1, Ms. W_2
Polygon construction.

Points In and around Polygons, Mr. W_1
The sum of the distances from a point in the interior of an equilateral triangle to its side is a constant.

OTHER TOPICS

An Application of "What-If-Not" in Problem Solving, Ms. A_2
Exploring the construction of squares on the sides of a quadrilateral and connecting the centers of opposite squares.

Some Observations on Multiplication Tables, Ms. L_1
"Mod"ifying multiplication.

Are the Field Axioms Independent?, Mr. W_2
The formula $a + b = b + a$ is proved from the other field axioms.

A Curriculum Unit on Prime Numbers, Ms. W_1
A teaching unit on prime numbers.

2. Table of Contents of Board X

Butterfly Problem, by Ms. M_1

One cannot but help to be intrigued by the development of Ms. M_1's problem. One gets a good insight into her thought processes concerning the solution of this very difficult problem of geometry.

Butterfly Problem Re-visited, by Mr. O_1

Letter to Mr. O_1 from Board.

A well organized description of several methods used in attacking the butterfly problem. These same methods can be applied to a large number of difficult geometry problems.

A Generating Formula for Integral Solutions to $a^2 + b^2 = c^2$, by Mr. G_1

This paper gives a well motivated discussion on a formula for primitive Pythagorean triplets. The writer takes you step-by-step through his discovery of the result. The reader will especially enjoy the clarity as well as the content.

Some Random Notes on Pythagorean Numbers, by Mr. G_2

Letter to Mr. G_2.

Although this paper is entitled "Some Random Notes on Pythagorean Numbers," one finds very many deep number theoretic results in it. This is a must paper for those interested in number theory.

Untitled, by Mr. G_3

Letter to Mr. G_3.

Many problems are deeply related to each other. Here is an exposition relating fractional solutions of the Pythagorean Formula to the circle. You will also notice the dependence of each topic on Pythagorean Numbers.

On the Quadratic Triplets, by Ms. H_3

Letter to Mr. H_3 from Board.

An empirical approach has revealed several conjectures about rational solutions of the Pythagorean Formula. Some are quite surprising, and you may enjoy investigating them further.

Some Interesting Problems, Books and Articles.

Untitled, by Ms. M_1

The reader is given the pieces used in transforming a parallelogram into a square and shown how these pieces are used in a proof of the Pythagorean theorem.

Variations on a Theme by Pythagoras, by Mr. G_1

This paper looks at three twists on the old theme. Integer-sided 60° triangles, integer points on the ellipse, and the imperfect Pythagorean triplets generated by relations of the form $a^2 + b^2 = c^2 + k$ are investigated and some surprising relationships are found.

Minimum Path Problems, by Mr. G_1

Can we find a method which will help us to find the minimum path inside any polygon?

What If Not "What-If-Not," by Ms. H_3

A critical analysis and discussion of the "What-If-Not" approach to problem posing.

The Golden Section, by Mr. H_1

Showing a method of building a golden section segment using tangent and secant to a circle. The second part of the paper, showing extension to any segment, is needlessly involved. A much more direct method exists.

Circular Reasoning, by Mr. G_2

A general problem with tangent circles involves some rather fancy reasoning, but a few of the specific cases are solvable with very elementary high-school geometry and a brief algebraic manipulation. One is solvable with little more than a clever elementary school trick.

Matrices & Transformations: The Problem of Undoing, by Mr. G_1, Ms. H_3, Ms. M_2, Mr. M_1, and Mr. G_2

Linear transformations have geometric interpretations, and can also be related to the algebra of matrices. This paper describes those relationships.

A collection of interesting problems that have come up in class, by the editorial board of Journal π.

Excerpts from "Published" Articles

The following are some brief excerpts from articles published in the class journals which convey something not only of the mathematical investigation, but of the personal reflective spirit that some students were able to capture in the course—an introspective stance that was difficult for many students to express. We end the collection with an editorial which is not only reflective but self-serving (from our point of view). Perhaps it will counterbalance some of our words of caution and will inspire others to venture into a course of this type.

Final Group Paper on Pythagorean Triples, Mr. A_1, Ms. L_1, Mr. B_2

"Working in the full class group Tuesday I found to be frustrating. My mind seemed to be reacting slowly to the suggestions and I felt that I wanted to follow through on some of the conjectures but my train of thought was constantly being interrupted. Obviously some stimulation was being generated since the thought that $3^2 - 1^2 = 8$ came to me later as I was driving. In contrast on Wednesday in the small group, I found myself leaping from one line of reasoning to another without feeling frustrated. Was this due to the smallness of the group? Was it because the conjectures of the group were less diverse? Was it because I had an incubation period for the problem? Was it because I felt responsibility for seeing that the group was productive? Whatever the reason, the ideas seemed to come more readily in the small group than in the large class setting and my mind seemed more able to respond to the stimulus of suggestions from other members of the group. Might the key lie in a genetic or conditioned learning strategy? Perhaps I naturally prefer convergent thinking (successive scanning) and also tend toward reflective rather than impulsive responses in problem solving . . .''

"What-If-Not," Pat Burke[1]

"The 'What-If-Not' articles tantalized my curiosity to ask the question, 'What-If-Not' a square geoboard? Therefore, I constructed six geoboards . . . Using these new geoboards, I posed new questions:

1. How many triangles can be constructed?
2. What types of triangles can be constructed? . . .

Next I put several geoboards together and formed:

3. Parallelogram-rhombus, using two of the boards . . .
4. Is there any convex shape I can make from five triangular geoboards?

I next modified the attribute that a geoboard be flat . . .''

A New Way to Look at a Circle, Ms. B$_1$

"The following is an extension of my 'What-If-Not' paper on the equation $x^2 + y^2 = 25$. I asked myself the question, What-If-Not this equation were graphed on regular coordinate axes? After having initially found some surprising discoveries, I become really interested in this and investigated further. What evolved, it seems to me, is the seed of a unit not only on graphing, but on circles and ellipses . . . and perhaps with a little more imagination one might be able to incorporate parabolas and hyperbolas too. I'll explain this

---

[1]We intentionally list Ms. Burke's name here. Both Ms. Burke and her husband were tragically killed in a traffic accident in 1979. We include this short excerpt from one of her pieces in the spirit of fond remembrance.

aspect of the paper further after you have been exposed to some of my ideas. . . .''

What If Not "What-If-Not"?, Ms. H₁

"The 'What-If-Not' approach to mathematical situations is intriguing . . . mostly because it is not clear whether it is really rich or fake rich. In this paper, I am not sure whether I am criticizing, asking for better definitions or talking about other possible use. I am probably doing all three.

The stated objectives of the approach are to (1) encourage teachers and students to pose new questions about mathematical phenomena and (2) provide a model or technique for posing new questions. Hopefully this will lead to new curriculum ideas. Many of my questions crystallized as I tried to apply the What-If-Not technique to generate curriculum ideas for a 10th grade geometry class. I am using that attempt to illustrate the questions . . .''

Under Observation, Mr. M₁

"In our last session, I elected to be one of the observed. I felt pressure to produce while being observed and hence to alleviate some pressure I tried making myself comfortable.

Initially the squaring problem looked routine, however, it did not prove to be routine and simple. After the session, I noted the following as my strategies for solving the problem:

1. *Obvious answer.* If the answer was obvious, it could be seen quickly (insight required). I had NO LUCK.
2. *Trial and error.* Make intelligent guesses and test solutions. NO LUCK again.
3. *Bulldozer method.* Since answer was not obvious, search for a pattern by bulldozing out more numbers and discover a generator. NO LUCK.
4. *Normal approach.* Look for a generalization by algebraic representation. NO LUCK.

Later when I worked further on the problem, I noted the following strategies:

5. What cannot work? Are there numbers that cannot work? Why?
6. A re-look through algebra and a formalized approach (insight).
7. Search for a pattern among selected components, i.e., break problem up into smaller parts that may be related (insight).
8. Formalize any observations and patterns. . . .''

Editorial, Ms. H$_5$ of the Phantom Board

"This course has made me more aware of the value of trial and error. Since I have been so conditioned to proving and disproving abstract concepts, I almost forgot the interesting questions and conjectures that can come out of trial and error. Examining many aspects of a problem has enabled me to have more insight into simple problems.

Working with the Pythagorean triples has given me information that I have already used in my senior classes. Enriching ideas or comments add to the interest of a course.

I have always been aware of the versatility of math, but now I stress this idea more in my classes.

I have also observed in my classes that most average high school students rely heavily on the teacher as the main source of information. If they have confidence in your mathematical ability, they believe almost every concept presented to them by you. I would assume that in advanced classes, the students would challenge the teacher more.

This course has been the most interesting and informative math education course that I have enrolled in here. This is the sixth math education course I've taken (two in undergraduate school and three in graduate school) and the first that has challenged me and forced me to think about my role as an educator."

SUMMARY

We hope that this brief description together with a few short excerpts have given you some insight into possible ways of incorporating some of our problem-generating ideas into classroom teaching. Even if you do not have an opportunity to employ them in teaching, however, we hope that some of what we have proposed will influence your thinking and learning—that it will enable you to understand in a more tentative mode what others propose as firm and fixed, and will provide schemes for "making it your own."

In most contexts within which learning proceeds in a school setting, one who is "pumped" with the "accepted" way of seeing and doing things is frequently discouraged from asking questions like:

- What do we believe it means to think?
- What do we believe we personally learn from our abortive efforts?
- What do we believe our responsibility ought to be to our colleagues?

We find that unless they are given the encouragement, time and space to reflect on such personal and intellectual matters, our students go about their business with more information but less wisdom than they ought to settle for.

If you teach, but cannot offer a course in problem posing exclusively, you may be able to incorporate either *some* of the problem generation ideas or perhaps *some* of the organizational ideas suggested by the metaphor of student as editorial board member. Although in this chapter we have suggested the metaphor as a mechanism for achieving some of the problem posing goals, each of these activities does have the potential for independent existence. One can certainly teach a course on problem generation without using editorial boards, and one can organize a course around editorial boards in the absence of problem generation as a focus.

8

Conclusion

A LOOK BACK

We have presented a rationale and set of strategies for the activity of problem generation and have tried to establish that essentially no understanding can take place without some effort at problem generation.

In chapter 3, we indicated how even a conservative conception of problem generation can both inform us of our preconceptions and widen our perspective. Although the strategies introduced in the chapter are useful for generating problems in which we "accept the given," they can be incorporated into "challenging the given" (the "What-If-Not" phase) as well. You may wish to look back on some of your favorite "What-If-Not" activities to determine where you did or might superimpose some of the tactics in chapter 3. To what extent did you make observations or, indeed, create conjectures, in addition to (or as a precursor of) generating questions, a part of our Level III activity? Further, what questions attempted to get at the internal character of what you were investigating? Which were geared to its external character? Were the questions framed in such a way that they required an exact answer, or was an approximation allowable (or perhaps even encouraged)? Did you ask questions of a pseudo-historical nature on the modified attributes? What questions from our handy list did you find useful? What new questions did you add to the handy list after the "What-If-Not" experience?

We hope the "What-If-Not" activity of chapters 4 and 5 has provided you with a vivid picture of an interesting irony—that we understand something best in the context of changing it. We also hope that it has given you an added sense of your own power as well. The strategies presented should help you appreciate that the generation of questions is not exclusively the task of textbook writers, teachers or other people in authority.

Just as you may enjoy returning to these chapters in an effort to re-examine the question-asking strategies of chapter 3, you will probably be surprised by how much more you are capable of uncovering now than when you began the journey. The achievement has been a significant one because, as we have suggested, merely seeing things that can be varied is not as easy as you might expect. Certainly, experience with the "What-If-Not" strategy will positively affect most people's ability to see phenomena as capable of modification that they had not so seen before. Yet there are many important factors in addition to an ability to see what resides in an object. Why is it that Eskimos see many different varieties of snow, and nomads can discriminate among hundreds of different kinds of camels? Even the most perceptive people in our modern technological society cannot see more than a limited variety of each of these. We are all affected by experience, by cultural experience, by special needs and by what we expect to see as well.[1]

PROBLEM POSING AND MATH ANXIETY

In addition, we are affected by a host of emotional factors which might impede or encourage problem generation—factors such as praise by, fear of, or threat from others. With regard to such emotional factors, there is an interesting twist, a possible "chicken and egg" problem which is in need of further clarification and empirical investigation. Many people are interested in finding out why mathematics engenders so much fear in people who may otherwise be highly competent and functional. What are the causes of the "disease"—a disease referred to as mathophobia or math anxiety—and how might it be cured? Though there are many approaches to this (as yet) vaguely defined problem, we know of very little which *starts* with problem generation as a primary means of trying to understand and confront the fear. There is good reason to believe that problem generation might be a critical ingredient in confronting math anxiety because the *posing* of problems or asking of questions is potentially less threatening than answering them. The reason is in part a logical one. That is, when you *ask* a question, the responses "right" or "wrong" are inappropriate, though that category is paramount for *answers* to questions . Of course, it is logically possible to claim that some questions are good and others bad, or at least that some questions are better than others, and so perhaps the potential to be intimidated by it all still remains.

-----

[1]For a philosophical discussion of this phenomenon, see Kuhn, Thomas J., *The Structure of Scientific Revolutions,* University of Chicago Press, 1970. A psychological analysis is provided by Bruner, Jerome S. and Postman, Leo, "On the Perception of Incongruity: A Paradigm," *Journal of Personality,* XVIII, 1949, pp. 206–233.

But as we have seen in chapters 4 and 5, as soon as we begin to deviate from standard and well-trodden knowledge (as in the case of "What-If-Not-ing"), it is frequently difficult to judge the value of a question. Sometimes we do not know how simple, revealing, delightful, or foolish a question is until *after* considerable analysis has taken place. Since "What-If-Not-ing" leads so naturally to non-standard curriculum, there is no longer the kind of immediacy of personal judgment or judgment from others that is so often intimidating.

A second reason that the threat of judgment becomes tempered in problem generation is that, as we pointed out in chapters 4 and 5, something that is silly or even meaningless may be a hair's breadth away from something that is significant.

We are suggesting that though there are many factors that may impede our ability to even see things to modify in a "What-If-Not" spirit, the activity of problem generation might be one important element in confronting one of these factors: the fear of mathematics itself. How the potential relationship between fear of mathematics and seeing factors to vary works out for students of different interest and ability will require some empirical research that would be well worth conducting.

But each of us can do research of sorts on ourselves without waiting for the results of a specialist. We might ask ourselves what kinds of encounters eventually enable us to see the potential for modification when the "object" to be modified was not apparent on initial inquiry. Though we have not devoted a special section to it, at various places throughout the book we have reflected on our own use of devices of thought which are generally more closely associated with poetry and art than with mathematics. We have spoken about how it is that we caught ourselves making use of imagery or metaphor while engaging in "What-If-Not" activity. We have indicated in chapter 4, for example, how "striving" was an image that enabled us to push towards a new way of conceiving of multiplication.

PROBLEM POSING AND CO-OPERATION

We can, however, do a lot more than reflect upon our use of such devices as an effort to improve our capacity for problem generation. An important thing we can do is to learn to work productively and perhaps less competitively with others. Frequently others see what we neglect to see. If the links between problem generation and problem solving are as interdependent logically as we have claimed in our discussion in chapter 6, and if the talent to operate well within these two realms is less tightly linked, then there is good reason to find ways for people with these different talents to interact.[2]

---

[2]See Getzels, Jacob W. and Jackson, Philip W. *Creativity and Intelligence,* New York: John Wiley and Sons, 1962, for an empirical argument that the two talents may be more diverse than is generally believed.

In Chapter 7 we point to one model for having people draw on each other's strengths—a model that is useful in educational settings, though we certainly need to find models and ways of applying them in other contexts as well. Our model is that of student as editorial board member. With regard to that model we suggest many activities that might take place in an educational setting within which both creative and critical judgments can be encouraged. The general conception of organizing classwork around several editorial boards (each of which creates its own policy of acceptance and produces a journal based upon submission of articles by colleagues) is one that not only provides an atmosphere for encouraging problem generation, but fosters a spirit of adventure, intellectual excitement and class unity as well.

In closing, it is worth stressing that problem generation is not merely a new fad to be adopted in school settings in the same way that programmed instruction or team teaching washed over the scene. Problem generation has the potential to redefine in a radical way who it is that is in charge of one's education. As students are encouraged to raise questions and to pose problems of their own, rather than to merely "receive" the so-called wisdom of the ages, they take a new and more active role in their own learning. Exploration along the lines we have advocated in this book also re-conceptualizes the concept of error or mistake. As one begins to adopt a "What-If-Not" mentality, then instances which falsify desired generalization raise whole new possibilities for investigation rather than threaten our search.[3]

But a problem posing education has even deeper potential than what has been described so far. As a society, we are in need of seeing and standing on end many of the assumptions and conclusions that have been accepted for generations—at least as a heuristic for generating new perspectives, and to test the meaning of old ones. What if we assumed as a society that war was not inevitable? What if we assumed that the most distant foreigner shared the same fundamental beliefs and feelings that we did? Where would that leads us? What would be the implications? What would be our responsibilities?

We certainly have to be clearer about the framing of these issues than we have been so far in order to begin to make sense out of them. However, unless we begin to pose problems that challenge some of the so-called wisdom of the ages, we are most certainly doomed as a civilization. As in the case of turning Euclid's parallel postulate inside out and asking "What-If-Not" with regard to a 2000-year-old assumption, we need at the very least to entertain the possibility that our most cherished beliefs might not only be wrong but be meaningless as well!

---

[3]See, for example, Raffaella Borasi, "Exploring Mathematics Through the Analysis of Errors," *For the Learning of Mathematics,* Vol. 7, No. 3, 1987, 1–8, and Lawrence N. Meyerson, "Mathematical Mistakes," *Mathematics Teaching,* No. 76, 1976, 38–40.

Bibliography

Adams, J. L. (1974). *Conceptual blockbusting*. San Francisco, CA: Freeman.

Agre, G. P. (1982). The concept of problem. *Educational Studies, 13* (2), 121–142.

Becker, H. (1986). *Writing for social scientists*. Chicago, IL: University of Chicago Press.

Blake, R. N. (1984). 1089: An example of generating problems. *Mathematics Teacher, 77* (1), 14–19.

Borasi, R. (1987). Exploring mathematics through the analysis of errors. *For the Learning of Mathematics, 7* (3), 1–8.

Brown, S. I. (1965). Of 'prime' concern: What domain. *Mathematics Teacher, 58* (5), 402–407.

Brown, S. I. (1966). Multiplication, addition and duality. *Mathematics Teacher, 59* (6), 543–550.

Brown, S. I. (1968). Prime pedagogical schemes. *American Mathematical Monthly, 75* (6), 660–664.

Brown, S. I. (1971). Rationality, irrationality and surprise. *Mathematics Teaching, 55,* 13–19.

Brown, S. I. (1974). A musing on multiplication. *Mathematics Teaching, 61,* 26–30.

Brown, S. I. (1975). A new multiplication algorithm: On the complexity of simplicity. *Arithmetic Teacher, 22* (7), 546–554.

Brown, S. I. (1978). *Some prime comparisons*. Reston, VA: National Council of Teachers of Mathematics.

Brown, S. I. (1981). Sharon's 'Kye'. *Mathematics Teaching, 94,* 11–17.

Brown, S. I. (1984). The logic of problem generation: From morality and solving to deposing and rebellion. *For The Learning of Mathematics, 4*(1), 9–20.

Brown, S. I. (1987). *Student generations*. Arlington, MA: Consortium for Mathematics and its Applications (COMAP).

Brown, S. I., & Walter, M. I. (1970). What-if-not? An elaboration and second illustration. *Mathematics Teaching, 51,* 9–17.

Brown, S. I., & Walter, M. I. (1972). The role of the specific and general cases in problem posing and solving. *Mathematics Teaching, 59,* 52–54.

Brown, S. I., & Walter, M. I. (1988). Problem posing in mathematics education. *Questioning Exchange, 2* (2), 123–131.

Bruner, J. S., & Postman, L. (1949). On the perception of incongruity: A paradigm. *Journal of Personality, 18* (2), 206–223.

Burton, L. (1986). *Thinking things through: Problem solving in mathematics.* Oxford, Basil Blackwell.

Cassidy, C., & Hodgson, B. R. (1982). Because a door has to be open or closed. *Mathematics Teacher, 75* (2), 155–158.

Davis, R. (1973). The misuse of educational objectives. *Educational Technology, 13,* 34–36.

Dewey, J. (1957). *Reconstruction in philosophy.* Boston: Beacon Press.

Dillon, J. T. (1988). Levels of problem finding vs. problem solving. *Questioning Exchange, 2* (2), 105–115.

Eves, H. (1969). *An introduction to the history of mathematics* New York: Holt, Rinehart and Winston.

Ewing, D. (1977, December). Discovering your problem solving style. *Psychology Today,* pp. 69–73, 138, 140.

Freire, P. (1970). *Pedagogy of the oppressed.* New York: Seabury Press.

Gardiner, A. (1987). *Discovering mathematics: The art of investigation.* New York: Oxford University Press.

Gardiner, A. (1987). *Mathematical puzzling.* Oxford: Oxford University Press.

Gardner, M. (1965, May). Mathematical games. *Scientific American,* pp. 120–126.

Gardner, M. (1969). The multiple fascination of the Fibonacci sequence. *Scientific American,* pp. 116–120.

Getzels, J. W., & Jackson, P. W. (1962). *Creativity and intelligence.* New York: Wiley.

Gowin, D. B. (1981). *Educating.* Ithaca, NY: Cornell University Press.

Heath, T. L. (1956). *Euclid's elements.* New York: Dover.

Hoffer, A. R. (1979). *Geometry.* Menlo Park, CA: Addison Wesley.

Hofstadter, D. (1980). *Gödel, Escher and Bach: The Eternal Golden Braid.* New York: Vintage.

Jones, D. L., & Shaw, K. L. (1988). Reopening the equilateral triangle problem: What happens if . . . . *Mathematics Teacher, 81* (8), 634–639.

Jungck, J. R. (1985). A problem posing approach to biology education. *The American Biology Teacher, 47* (5), 264–266.

Kissane, B. V. (1988). Mathematical investigations: Description, rationale, and example. *Mathematics Teacher, 81* (7), 520–528.

Kuhn, T. J. (1970). *The structure of scientific revolutions.* Chicago: University of Chicago Press.

Kuper, M. & Walter, M. (1976). From edges to solids. *Mathematics Teaching, 74,* 20–23.

Loomis, E. (1968). *The pythagorean proposition.* Reston, VA. National Council of Teachers of Mathematics.

Martin, J. (1970). *Explaining, understanding and teaching.* New York: McGraw-Hill.

Meyerson, L. N. (1976). Mathematical mistakes. *Mathematics Teaching, 76,* 38–40.

Moise, E. (1965). Activity and motivation in mathematics. *American Mathematical Monthly, 72* (4), 407–412.

Niven, I., & Zuckerman, H. (1967). Lattice points and polygonal area. *American Mathematical Monthly, 74* (10), pp. 1195–1200.

Perkins, D. N. (1986). *Knowledge as design.* Hillsdale, NJ: Lawrence Erlbaum Associates.

Polya, G. (1973). *How to solve it.* Princeton, NJ: Princeton University Press.

Polya, G. (1967). *Mathematical discovery: On understanding, learning and teaching problem solving* (Vol. 1). New York: Wiley.

Polya, G. (1954). *Mathematics and plausible reasoning.* Princeton, NJ: Princeton University Press.

Potok, C. (1983). *In the beginning.* New York: Knopf.

Schmidt, P. A. (1975). A non-simply connected geoboard-based on the What-If-Not idea. *Mathematics Teacher, 68* (5), 384–388.

Schön, D. A. (1983). *The reflective practitioner.* New York: Basic Books.

Stein, M. L., Ulam, S. M., & Wells, M. B. (1964). A visual display of some properties of the distribution of primes. *American Mathematical Monthly, 71,* 515–520.

Toulmin, S. (1977). *Human Understanding*. Princeton, NJ: Princeton University Press.

Walter, M. (1968). Polyominoes, Milk Cartons and Groups. *Mathematics Teaching, 53*, 12–19.

Walter, M. (1969). A second example of informal geometry: Milk cartons. *Arithmetic Teacher, 16* (5), 368–370.

Walter, M. (1970a). A few steps down the path of a locus problem. *Mathematics Teaching, 53*, 23–25.

Walter, M. (1970b). *Boxes, squares and other things: A teacher's guide to a unit on informal geometry*. Reston, VA: National Council of Teachers of Mathematics.

Walter, M. (1980). Frame geometry: An example in posing and solving problems. *The Arithmetic Teacher*, 16–18. First published in *The Oregon Mathematics Teacher*, October 1979, pp. 19–23.

Walter, M. (1981a). Do we rob students of a chance to learn? *For the Learning of Mathematics, 1* (3), 16–18.

Walter, M. (1981b). Exploring a Rectangle Problem. *Mathematics Magazine, 54* (3), 131–134.

Walter, M. (1985). The day all textbooks disappeared. *Mathematics Teaching, 112*, 8–11.

Walter, M. (1987a). Generating problems from almost anything: Part 1. *Mathematics Teaching, 120*, 3–7.

Walter, M. (1987b). Generating problems from almost anything: Part 2. *Mathematics Teaching, 121*, 2–6.

Walter, M. (1989). Curriculum topics through problem posing. *Mathematics Teaching, 128*, 23–25.

Walter, M., & Brown, S. (1969). "What-If-Not." *Mathematics Teaching, 46*, 38–45.

Walter, M. I., & Brown, S. I. (1971). Missing ingredients in teacher training: One remedy. *American Mathematical Monthly, 78* (4), 399–404.

Walter, M. I., & Brown, S. I. (1977). Problem posing and problem solving: An illustration of their interdependence. *Mathematics Teacher, 70* (1), 4–13.

Yaglom, I., & Yaglom, A. (1967). *Challenging mathematical problems* (Vol. 2). San Francisco: Holden-Day.

Author Index

Subject Index